Human Rights and the Courts

BRINGING JUSTICE HOME

Human Rights and the Courts
Bringing Justice Home

Published 1999 by
WATERSIDE PRESS
Domum Road
Winchester SO23 9NN
Telephone or Fax 01962 855567
E-mail:watersidepress@compuserve.com

Copyright

Paul Ashcroft
Fiona Barrie
Chris Bazell
Audrey Damazer
Richard Powell
George Tranter

ISBN Paperback 1 872 870 80 5

Cataloguing-in-Publication Data A catalogue record for this book can be obtained from the British Library

Printing and binding Antony Rowe Ltd, Chippenham

Cover design John Good Holbrook Ltd, Coventry. Front cover illustration by Peter Cameron. The story of how Peter Cameron—who started painting while serving a prison sentence and won a Koestler Award (going on to become a judge for those awards and a Koestler trustee)—turned his life around is one of a number of 'Tales of Hope and Regeneration' featured in *Going Straight* (Waterside Press, 1999). He is now a freelance artist and screen printer and can be contacted at The Hub, 9 to 13 Berry Street, Liverpool. Telephone 0151 709 0889.

Human Rights and the Courts

BRINGING JUSTICE HOME

Paul Ashcroft
Fiona Barrie
Chris Bazell
Audrey Damazer
Richard Powell
George Tranter

WITH A FOREWORD BY
LORD IRVINE OF LAIRG, LORD CHANCELLOR

Produced under the auspices of the Justices' Clerks' Society

Edited by Bryan Gibson

WATERSIDE PRESS
WINCHESTER

Foreword

This Government came into office with a commitment to 'bring rights home' by incorporating the European Convention on Human Rights into the domestic law of the United Kingdom. This has been achieved through the Human Rights Act 1998 which represents a key stage in the evolution of the law and constitution of Great Britain.

It is important that all who serve in the courts—whether as Judges, magistrates or legal advisers—are at the forefront of these developments and fully equipped to understand new ways of thinking about the rights of individuals.

The European Convention itself arose from a need to protect people who might be vulnerable to the actions and decisions of the state (including public authorities and the courts) by introducing basic standards below which no laws or procedures should fall. The courts must ensure that these basic human rights are safeguarded and upheld through decisions, practices and procedures, something which may require a reassessment of the way in which decisions are arrived at. The Convention will also determine how courts operate in relation to a broad range of responsibilities—including the way they serve the public.

Human Rights and the Courts: Bringing Justice Home has been produced in conjunction with the Lord Chancellor's Department and the Judicial Studies Board. It has been written by members of the Working Group which produced the national Human Rights training for lay magistrates, justices' clerks and court legal advisers. It provides solid background information to complement and reinforce that training. I hope all magistrates will add to their understanding of this vital new development in domestic law by finding time to read, consider and refer to the straightforward account of Human Rights contained in this book. It avoids unnecessary technicalities and emphasises the positive task which lies ahead for all who serve in our courts.

Lord Irvine of Lairg
Lord Chancellor
October 1999

Human Rights and the Courts: Bringing Justice Home was devised in consultation with the Lord Chancellor's Department and Judicial Studies Board, and produced under the auspices of the Justices' Clerks' Society. The authors—all experienced lawyers holding senior positions in the Magistrates' Courts Service—were members of the Working Group which produced the national Human Rights training materials for magistrates and their legal advisers.

Human Rights and the Courts
Bringing Justice Home

CONTENTS

Acknowledgements

Very many people have contributed to this book—written at the same time that we were working on the various training materials for lay magistrates and professional staff in the courts—in order that we could validate the straightforward account which follows against the mass of often complex law, information and other data which makes up the full subject matter of human rights and the courts. The six of us and our editor wish to express sincere thanks to all concerned.

Paul Ashcroft
Fiona Barrie
Chris Bazell
Audrey Damazer
Richard Powell
George Tranter
Bryan Gibson

September 1999

CHAPTER 1

Introduction

The Human Rights Act 1998, which comes into force on 2 October 2000, has been described as probably the most important piece of constitutional legislation this century. The significance of the Act cannot be overstated. What it does—in the words of the government's original consultation paper—is to 'bring rights home' (which we have translated into a judicial context via the sub-title of this book, *Bringing Justice Home*). The rights referred to are those set out in the European Convention on Human Rights and Fundamental Freedoms, usually shortened to 'European Convention on Human Rights'. The Human Rights Act 1998 incorporates the Convention into the law of the United Kingdom and provides for those rights to be directly enforceable in our national courts for the first time.

THE EUROPEAN CONVENTION

In the immediate post-war period the Council of Europe was established by the governments of Western Europe with the intention of creating an international barrier to state tyranny as had existed on the continent for many years. One of the first tasks completed by the Council of Europe was the drawing up of a set of universal human rights designed to establish a minimum standard of protection for all citizens in Europe against the kind of state behaviour which had characterised the fascist decades. These rights were then proclaimed in the European Convention on Human Rights and Fundamental Freedoms, agreed by the Council of Europe in Rome in November 1950—a document based largely upon the Universal Declaration of Human Rights which had been issued in 1948 by the United Nations. The European Convention on Human Rights (further abbreviated in this book to 'the Convention') came into force in international law in 1953.

The right of individuals to petition the Court of Human Rights
Originally, the Convention only permitted states to take action against other states which they claimed had violated the Convention. Such actions were brought before an international court called the European Court of Human Rights (referred to in this book simply as 'the Court'). The Court sits at Strasbourg and is staffed by legal luminaries and judges drawn from the member states of the Council of Europe. The Convention

and its rules of procedure also provided for states to allow private individuals to bring actions in the Court against governments for breaches of the rights set out in a number of Articles of the Convention. In 1966 the United Kingdom recognised this right of individual petition with respect to its own citizens and since then many cases have been brought against the UK.

What are Human Rights?

The Convention contains a series of 'Articles', each laying down a minimum standard for the protection of a particular human right. Thus, e.g. in a largely judicial context Article 6 proclaims 'the right to a fair trial' and Article 7 'no punishment without law'. However, what we currently understand about such matters may be something quite different to what is envisaged by the Convention or what the Court may require when interpreting these guarantees. It may also be that a Convention right which we would not at first sight think was particularly relevant to the everyday business of the courts—such as Article 8 'the right to respect for private and family life'—requires a fresh approach to be adopted with regard to some existing (not to say cherished) procedures. This, in essence, is what this book is about: the need to adopt new ways of thinking about judicial (and other public) decisions, a different 'mind-set'. This will become clearer after reading *Chapter 2* which sets out a number of key principles, or 'concepts', developed by the Court in Strasbourg and which must be borne in mind at all times—such as *proportionality, equality of arms* and *positive obligation*—and after looking at the individual Articles in *Chapter 3*.

Articles and 'Protocols' distinguished

The main body of articles within the Convention has been supplemented since 1950 by a series of Protocols containing additional rights or enhancements of established standards. All the Articles and Protocols adopted by the UK are included in a schedule to the 1998 Act and for convenience these are set out in full in *Chapter 3* with a commentary attached to each.

Fundamental nature of the Articles and Protocols

Generally speaking the essence of each and every Convention right is that it is one which is:

- inherent

- inalienable; and

- universal.

The rights represent the freedoms and standards which must be recognised by democratic society in order to meet the basic conditions for civilisation. In terms of what a citizen can expect from his or her government the standards in the Convention are *minimum* standards. In other words, they represent a floor, not a ceiling—and therefore it can be expected that states which are more advanced in terms of their appreciation of human rights and which have liberal, democratic processes will ensure that national laws, procedures and practices establish even higher goals.

As to the inherent quality of human rights, they are not granted by a state. Rather, each and every person possesses them as a direct consequence of his or her humanity—at birth, through life and into death, regardless of age, nationality, sex, race or other status (indeed, Article 14 provides that such rights shall be enjoyed without discrimination). Each individual is fully entitled to have his or her rights respected and to have effective recourse to law whenever a state transgresses, interferes with or attempts to transgress or interfere with them. The preamble to the Universal Declaration of Human Rights (on which the Convention is largely based: see p.9) proclaims:

> Whereas recognition of the inherent dignity and of the equal and inalienable rights of all members of the human family is the foundation of freedom, justice and peace in the world.

> Whereas disregard and contempt for human rights have resulted in barbarous acts which have outraged the conscience of mankind, and the advent of a world in which human beings shall enjoy freedom of speech and belief and freedom from fear and want has been proclaimed as the highest aspiration of the common people.

TERMINOLOGY

It will be clear already that there is a good deal of new terminology to master (all explained at appropriate points in this book). There are some terms which occur repeatedly and others which are easily misdescribed or referred to in a loose way. The note, *When reading this book* overleaf sets out a few abbreviations which we have used for items central to an outline of the subject. We have used these consistently—and would encourage anyone dealing with human rights to ensure that their descriptions are clear to other people, if necessary by explaining what is meant (Article 10 proclaims 'the right to freedom of expression' which includes 'the right to receive and impart information and ideas'). Similarly, it is essential to understand and refer accurately to the key concepts in *Chapter 2* and the Articles themselves in *Chapter 3*.

When reading this book

To avoid undue repetition and sustain the flow of the text the following shorthand descriptions are used throughout this work:

'the Convention': the Convention for the Protection of Human Rights and Fundamental Freedoms, often described more simply as the European Convention on Human Rights.[1] Other Conventions mentioned in the text are described by their full title.

'the 1998 Act': the Human Rights Act 1998

'the Court', 'the Court at Strasbourg' or simply 'Strasbourg': when Court appears with an upper case 'C' this means the European Court of Human Rights based in Strasbourg. If the word court has a lower case 'c' this means 'magistrates' court' (or, depending on the context, a national court in another country). But note that High Court, Divisional Court and Crown Court all appear in the text with an upper case 'C' following conventional usage. No confusion should arise because these courts are always given their full title.

'national court' or 'domestic court': A court which is *local* to an individual state (as opposed to the European Court of Human Rights in Strasbourg). The two descriptions are fully interchangeable and nothing whatsoever turns on using one description rather than the other. Both are used in the text in different sections of the book to reflect the way it will be in practice—depending on what e.g. advocates choose to say or which description is used in a ruling or other source of information. *All* English and Welsh courts are 'national' (or 'domestic') courts vis-à-vis Europe—and *whatever level* of court in this country is under discusion.

'national law' or 'domestic law': the *local* law of a state as opposed to the Convention. Again, the descriptions are interchangeable. Many references in the book are to institutions, rulings about, or the system or position 'in the UK'. The book deals specifically with England and Wales with regard national law in the courts.

Note The Human Rights Act 1998 uses precise wording (as all Acts of Parliament do). We have followed this but not to the extent of rendering the text 'overtechnical'. Definitions appear in various section of the Act, including section 21 headed 'Interpretation, etc.'.

---

[1] We have avoided 'ECHR' which could apply equally to the Convention or the Court. Schedule 4 of the 1998 Act ('Judicial Pensions') uses it for the latter.

HUMAN RIGHTS IN THE UNITED KINGDOM

Traditionally, the UK Parliament has been charged with protecting individual rights—including what are in essence human rights—with the common law doing this in instances where Parliament has failed or declined to do so. People may conduct themselves as they see fit unless Parliament or the common law has made certain conduct unlawful. But critically, under UK law, the rights of individuals arise as a consequence of the general law and the doctrine of the supremacy of Parliament, not as a result of anything inherent in the individual. In other words, UK citizens have not previously *enjoyed rights*—merely the *consequences* of legislative action and judicial decision-making.

Likewise, no single code exists in the UK setting out the nature or extent of an individual's rights. The absence of a Bill of Rights—a written constitution defining the limits of state authority and power—has long been a source of debate and for many people of criticism. The scale of this debate can be gleaned by considering the fact that it arose as long ago as 1215 in Magna Carta and continued through the Civil War between the King and Parliament up to the so-called Bill of Rights of 1688 and beyond.

Convention rights contrasted

As already indicated, the Convention imposed duties on the state but gave no direct redress to individuals. The right of individual petition granted by the UK government in 1966 at least offered the opportunity for an individual citizen to take the government to the Court in Strasbourg to account for its actions, but only after all national remedies were exhausted, and even then a finding against the state did not result in a change to national law.

In answer to these perceived deficiencies, ministers of state and judges of the higher courts in the UK reminded people that national law was generally in accord with the rights under the Convention, or that sufficient remedies existed in law to adequately protect the individual against the state. Sadly, the figures for actions against the UK government do not bear this out. Since the right of individual petition was granted over 6,000 applications have been made against the UK. Many have concerned breaches of the most important rights in the Convention and challenges have been mounted to both primary legislation (Acts of Parliament) and secondary legislation (statutory instruments etc.) (as to both of which see, generally, *Chapter 4*). In truth, the UK's record has been poor (although not the worst in Western Europe by any means). This fact became a subject of political interest in the 1980s and early 1990s and three attempts were made to bring forward private members Bills to give effect to the Convention—in 1987, 1994 and again in 1996. Then the Labour Party published, *Bringing Rights Home*, which led to the Human Rights Act 1998.

The Convention in the UK before the Human Rights Act 1998
Before implementation of the Human Rights Act 1998 in October 2000 there are very few occasions when it can be engaged by an individual to protect his or her rights. In summary, national courts have only turned to the Convention:

- as an aid to the construction of legislation where there is ambiguity: *R v. Secretary of State for the Home Department, ex parte Brind* [1991] 1 AC 696

- to assist in determining how to exercise judicial discretion: *Attorney-General v. Guardian Newspapers Ltd.* [1987] 1 WLR 1248; and

- to identify the scope of the common law: *Derbyshire County Council v. Times Newspapers Ltd.* [1992] QB 770.

Thus, national courts have (until the 1998 Act is in force) been unable to give direct effect to the broad spectrum of rights in the Convention because it had not been incorporated into UK law. Similarly national courts have been unable to reflect decisions of the Court. As the jurisprudence concerning the nature and extent of human rights grew, the likelihood of injustice arising in the UK increased. The case for incorporating the Convention into national law was never stronger.

THE HUMAN RIGHTS ACT 1998

In response to *Bringing Rights Home* and after detailed Parliamentary debate, the Human Rights Act 1998 was enacted to come into force on 2 October 2000. It is important to recognise at the outset that the 1998 Act does *not* in itself create new criminal offences or civil rights of action. Neither does it introduce any new substantive rules of procedure. It is not a codification of any part of existing national laws, which continue as before. What it does do is affect the way that existing laws, procedures and practices are applied—in summary in a way that is compatible with Convention rights. It also states what courts are to do if they believe that these national ways of doing things are not compatible with those rights. The Act (the main text of which is reproduced in *Appendix I* to this book) sets about 'bringing rights and justice home' in three ways:

- first, it requires all courts and tribunals *to take into account* the Convention and decisions by the institutions of the Convention (whether the Court of Human Rights, the Council or the now replaced Commission on Human Rights).

- second, the 1998 Act provides for national courts to read primary and secondary legislation in such a way that it is *compatible* with the Convention. In some cases this may mean that a national court is able to ignore *secondary* legislation or decisions of higher courts in the UK in order to protect rights guaranteed under the Convention.

- third, the legislation imposes a duty on *all* public authorities *to act compatibly* with the Convention—and it becomes a civil wrong for a public authority not to do this.

These three limbs create, in the view of government, an effective and meaningful raft of protections for the individual, without the need to create a special constitutional court or commission in the UK—although neither option has been completely ruled out.

The status of national courts

The 1998 Act imposes various duties on courts and public authorities which require further explanation:

- **Section 2(1)** of the Act requires a court (or tribunal) determining a question which has arisen in connection with a Convention right to *take into account* the judgements, decisions, declarations and opinions of the Court, the Commission and the Council. The words 'take into account' were chosen advisedly, to avoid the risk of national courts following European decisions as if they were binding on future cases in the way that rulings of the higher courts—'precedents'—are in English law. The status of precedent in relation to Convention methods of interpretation is discussed in more detail in *Chapter 2* and, where appropriate, in later chapters.

  The duty to take such matters into account extends to the interpretation of national legislation which must be read—so far as it is possible to do so—in a way that is *compatible* with the Convention. The practical implications of this duty to interpret legislation in accordance with the requirements of the 1998 Act and Convention is discussed in *Chapter 4*.

- **Section 6(1) and (3)** of the 1998 Act provide that it is unlawful for a public authority to act in a way that is *incompatible* with a

Convention right. Courts are expressly included within the definition of 'public authority'. Apart from applying to a court as normally understood, it also seems clear, e.g. that:

— an individual magistrate acting by virtue of his or her commission from the Sovereign and whether acting in the courtroom or in private (including when doing so at home) and, say, dealing with applications for search warrants or emergency protection orders, falls well within the requirement to 'act compatibly'

— justices' clerks and court clerks/legal advisers excercising judicial, quasi-judicial or administrative powers or carrying out any public responsibility are similarly affected

— the administrative part of the Magistrates' Courts Service will fall within the definition of public authority

— both a magistrate's court's committee (MCC) and its justices' chief executive will be classed as a public authority in that they exercise responsibilities which directly affect the public through the management of court services and public funds.

Accordingly, in each of the above situations the relevant court, committee, individual or individuals must act compatibly with the Convention—not only where the events in question occur *in court*, but also in any dealings 'behind the scenes' and with external organizations or other court users—and also internally, e.g. an MCC in relation to employment matters.

SOURCES OF HUMAN RIGHTS

The primary source of European human rights law under which courts and public authorities are required to act once the Convention is incorporated into English law is the body of case law, opinions and decisions built up over the last 50 years or so by the Court (and before it was abolished the European Commission on Human Rights). In 1998 the Commission was replaced by a full-time Court which assesses each application to decide whether it is admissible or manifestly unfounded. Once a junior court of three judges has decided that there is, in effect, a case to answer a full court of seven judges is constituted to hear the petition. Prior to this procedure the European Commission on Human Rights determined questions of admissibility and the results of these older decisions still form an important part of the overall jurisprudence.

Positive obligation

In addition to rights expressly set out in the Convention regard must be had to rights which are implied. The Convention is thus not a dry document simply listing rights which, so to speak, are writ in stone. Rather it has been described as 'a living instrument'. The rights—or to be more accurate the interpretation of those rights—changes over time as social conditions evolve and basic freedoms develop. Hand-in-hand with this principle is the concept of 'positive obligation' mentioned earlier in this chapter: that is to say the Convention may be silent on the nature or extent of a particular right, but the interpretation given to that silence by the Court may involve the creation of an obligation on a state to do something or to refrain from doing it. Such outcomes often involve a degree of imagination and lateral thinking on the part of the Court and, again, it is important to become used to a method of determination which is somewhat different to that which national courts may have been used to. This aspect is considered further in *Chapter 2*.

Children and minority groups

The Convention does not include any specific rights for children or a stand-alone right not to be discriminated against (as opposed to a requirement to secure other rights in the Convention without discrimination: Article 14). These are two of the most glaring omissions and whilst several of the other rights do engage children or touch upon discrimination it is hard to find European sources from which to draw firm conclusions.

However, other sources do exist in the wider world which may be of relevance and which can legitimately be taken into account. The Universal Declaration of Human Rights is likely to become an important source of principle. In *T v. United Kingdom* and *V v. United Kingdom* [1999] Crim. LR 579 ('the Bulger case') the Commission admitted a complaint regarding the trial procedure and subsequent detention of juveniles for murder in the UK. Several of the issues involved rights of children which are not explicit in the Convention. The Commission was prepared to look beyond Europe and quoted extensively from the United Nations Standard Minimum Rules for the Administration of Juvenile Justice (the Beijing Rules). Similarly the experiences of other countries, especially Commonwealth jurisdictions, may become a source of human rights law—reflecting the universality of Convention rights.

European law reports

A number of sources are available in the UK to research decisions of the the Court. The main reference works are likely to be the European Human Rights Reports (usually abbreviated to EHRR) and the European

Human Rights Law Review (EHRLR). Other series of domestic law reports carry occasional reports from the Court and as the impact of the Human Rights Act 1998 grows it seems likely that the coverage of decisions and judgements will increase.[2]

THE CONVENTION AND THE EUROPEAN UNION DISTINGUISHED

It sometimes seems that our lives are becoming more and more dominated by the notion of a 'Greater Europe'. Politicians, political activists, the business community and particularly the media focus a good deal of their comment upon Europe (often in fairly derogatory terms). Hopefully, a positive understanding of the Convention and its aims will mean that judges, magistrates and lawyers will not add their voices to any confusion. The European *Union* and the European *Convention* are not—as it might sometimes appear—one and the same thing. They have several features in common, but it is important to recognise the differences between them.

The European Union
The Union is the current manifestation of the European Community and the European Economic Community (EEC) before that. It comprises 15 member states working together under international treaty—the Treaty of Rome—towards an approximation of economic and social conditions. The Treaty of Rome established:

- a Commission

- a Council; and

- a Parliament.

The combined purpose was to initiate, debate, refine and legislate in areas of *economic* and *social* policy aimed at reducing and eventually abolishing barriers to the free movement of goods, services, workers and money within the European Union area. Disputes arising in the operation of Union legislation are resolved before the national courts assisted by the judgements of the European Court of Justice (which sits in Luxembourg and is not to be confused with the European Court of

---

[2] Both the Council and the Court have their own world-wide website. The European Court of Human Rights can be found at http://www.dhcour.coe.fr and the Council of Europe at http://www.coe.fr Further details of innovations in the United Kingdom may be found at the Human Rights icon at the Lord Chancellor's site at http://www.open.gov.uk/lcd

Human Rights which, as we have indicated, sits in Strasbourg—'the Court' which features in this book). Likewise, the European Union's Commission sits in Brussells and should not be mistaken for the European Commission on Human Rights which, as we have explained, is now defunct.

Why the confusion?

Some confusion exists because both the Convention and the Union create a legal order overseen by an international court often referred to simply and indiscriminately as 'the European Court'—as if they are one and the same (they are not, as already explained). Also, the Convention and Union each has its own Council of Ministers (often made up of the same individuals in practice) and the different functions discharged by each are not always accurately assigned by the media. The only truly shared characteristic of the Union and the Convention is that membership of the Union is conditional upon membership of the Council of Europe and adherence to the Convention. It follows from this that the Union itself also recognises the rights guaranteed under the Convention.

A PRACTICAL APPROACH TO HUMAN RIGHTS

This book is largely concerned with how fundamental human rights are 'brought home' in everyday practice in a judicial setting. The next chapter sets out the principles which need to be understood if guarantees are to be effective and *Chapter 3* the individual rights contained in the Articles of the Convention. The remainder of the book concentrates on showing what the position is in practice, including in the various jurisdictions of the magistrates' court and in relation to everyday matters such as 'evidence' and activities in and around the courtroom. The information about specialist jurisdictions should not be ignored by people who are not normally involved in them. Human rights do not operate in isolated compartments and there is a deal to learn from understanding how they apply across a broad front—which also helps to give a sense of their universal, inherent and inalienble qualities.

Chapter 1: Introduction

Some key points before proceeding to Chapter 2:

- this chapter is about a new approach to the role of courts in society. They are required to act in a way that is compatible with Convention rights.

- in order to do so they will need to be familiar with new terminology, new concepts—and how to apply them in practice

- human rights is a wide-ranging subject and there will be a need to consider judgements of the Court and in some instances other national or international human rights materials

- the Human Rights Act 1998 incorporates the Convention into domestic law, but this in itself does not create any new offences or procedures. It is in giving effect to Convention rights by interpreting national law compatibly with the Convention that things will change

- it is critically important to understand the terminology and the main concepts and to ensure that other people understand what is happening when the Convention is being considered.

CHAPTER 2

Jargon, Jargon, Jargon

As explained in *Chapter 1*, the incorporation of the Convention into the law of the United Kingdom demands that practitioners adopt a fresh way of thinking about and interpreting national law. The European dimension also brings with it new phrases and terminology—much of which will find its way into everyday language in and around the courtroom and soon become familiar. The most important new terms and phrases are explained in this chapter together with some examples to show what this may mean in practice.

ARTICLES

The Convention consists of a series of Articles (full details of each Article incorporated by the 1998 Act are set out in *Chapter 3*). Each Article describes a particular right. Generally speaking, someone seeking to rely on a Convention right will refer to the relevant Article as a shorthand way of identifying the right in question. Not all rights are the same in nature, quality or extent, nor to be found in the Convention itself. They may also exist in a number of Protocols or decisions of the Court, and— as indicated towards the end of *Chapter 1*—the scope of Convention rights may be affected by other sources in and beyond Europe.

Absolute rights
Some rights are *absolute*. They can never be departed from because they are fundamental to the rights of man. For example the right not to be subjected to torture or inhuman or degrading treatment or punishment in Article 3 is absolute. The use of such conduct by the state can never, no matter what the circumstances, be regarded as lawful.

Limited rights
Some rights are *limited* by the Convention. Within the scope of the limitation, an infringement of a guaranteed right may not amount to a contravention of the Convention. For example the right to life under Article 2(1) is subject to a limitation in Article 2(2) which states that deprivation of life is not to be regarded as a breach of the Convention where it results from the use of force which was no more than absolutely necessary in defence of a person from unlawful violence, to prevent escape from lawful detention or to effect an arrest or quell a riot or

insurrection. In *McCann v. United Kingdom* (1995) 21 EHRR 97 (the 'death on the rock' case in which suspected terrorists were shot dead on a garage forecourt in Gibraltar by British security agents) a breach of Article 2 was upheld by the Court against the UK. The state had failed to give adequate training or instructions to agents likely to use lethal force. This failure to plan and control went to the heart of whether the force used had been absolutely necessary.

Qualified rights

Some rights are *qualified* rights. The Convention permits such rights to be interfered with in certain circumstances or under certain conditions. Thus, e.g. under Article 8(1) an individual has a right to respect for his or here private and family life. Article 8(2) provides that a state may interfere with this right but only to the extent that such interference is in accordance with the law, pursues a limited number of defined objectives and is no more than is necessary in a democratic society. This last qualification introduces the concept of 'proportionality'—one of the most important of the other key concepts and principles explained in this chapter.

OTHER KEY CONCEPTS AND PRINCIPLES

Quite apart from the status of the right under consideration, one or more further concepts and principles may come into play:

Derogations and reservations

States may enter derogations against certain obligations under the Convention in times of war or other public emergency threatening the life of the nation. This allows that particular state not to comply with the Article in question to the legitimate extent of the derogation. Derogations must be specific and open to review, proportional (see below) to the threat and necessary to deal with the emergency in question. General derogations are *not* permitted. Neither is derogation in respect of the right to life (except arising from the lawful prosecution of war) or from the prohibitions against torture etc., slavery or retrospective penal legislation. The UK has entered derogations with respect to activities in Northern Ireland. Similarly, with reservations, which amount to a kind of conditional acceptance. The UK has entered a reservation with regard to the right to education. See *Chapter 3* for more details of both aspects.

Equality of arms

Equality of arms is a principle which was created by the Court in the case of *Neumeister v. Austria* (1968) 1 EHRR 91 to ensure that domestic legal processes, either civil or criminal do not place one party at a procedural disadvantage as against the other. Largely, the concept is a function of Article 6 which guarantees the right to a fair trial. There are many examples in the decisions of the Court which explain the concept of equality of arms. Thus, e.g. defence witnesses should be treated in the same way as prosecution witnesses; and each party should have the opportunity to test evidence adduced by the other.

Two examples of where equality of arms may be argued in a magistrate's court are, firstly, in the situation where someone has been arrested for breaching conditions of bail. A common practice is for the magistrate or magistrates to decide whether there has been a breach of bail by hearing an oral account by the prosecutor based on a written summary of the arresting police officer. Often, the defendant has no real opportunity to test that evidence or peruse it in advance—and may not even be given the opportunity to testify himself or herself. Such procedures seemingly place the defendant at a disadvantage.

Secondly, in purely summary cases there is no right for a defendant to have prior disclosure of the case against him or her, whereas for offences which are triable either way (i.e. in the Crown Court or magistrates' court) there is a right to advance information. Given that many summary offences carry the liability to a custodial sentence just as either way offences dealt with summarily do there is a procedural imbalance operating against the defendant which may amount to a breach of Article 6 (see further in *Chapter 3*).

Horizontality
As indicated in *Chapter 1*, the Human Rights Act 1998 requires all public authorities to act compatibly with the Convention. The rights in the Convention thus operate 'vertically' in that they affect relations between private individuals and public authorities. The concept of 'horizontality' suggests that the Convention can indirectly affect horizontal relationships between individual citizens. This occurs because courts and tribunals are defined as public authorities by section 6 of the 1998 Act. Thus when adjudicating, e.g. on a dispute between individuals courts need to act compatibly with the Convention—and relationships between individuals are affected indirectly. The 1998 Act does not say that a father must comply with the Convention in relations with his son—but if a dispute comes to court the decision must comply with the Convention and thus its principles will affect that 'horizontal' relationship.

Living instrument
The Convention was drafted in the early years of the first decade after the Second World War. Society was very different then compared to how

it is today. Older decisions of the Court (or Commission) reflected very much the choices of the day—not all of which would be relevant to a world entering the new millennium. The Court has recognised this aspect by referring to the Convention as a 'living instrument' and allowing rights to be interpreted in different ways over time.

The UK model

In the UK, decisions taken at any time in the past bind future courts. The doctrine of precedent means that courts must follow previous decisions of higher courts unless they have been overruled by a higher court or the facts of the earlier case are different from the facts of the later case and the principle involved can be distinguished from that in the earlier case. In this way the common law has developed relatively slowly and often with changes coming only after consideration at the highest judicial level—or where the issue has come before Parliament and 'amending' legislation has been enacted. The UK method has generally been that the court tries to interpret and apply Parliament's will and intentions. When doing so courts purport not to make law themselves. This again differs in relation to the Convention: see further under *Purposive Approach* later in this chapter.

The European model

The European model is different. Precedent plays a far less significant role and courts are free to develop the law to reflect the needs of society for the time being. Convention law follows the European model. Cases decided some time ago do not necessarily carry the same weight as they would under UK law.

Example of the 'living instrument' approach

A good example of the Convention as a living instrument concerns the recognition of the rights of gay couples. The Convention contains no specific rights for gay people but over time the Court has interpreted the Convention so as to create a sophisticated raft of gay rights. Presently the Court has begun to develop the rights of transsexuals, almost certainly an area barely considered by the authors of the Convention. Also, the Court has seldom shirked at the prospect of changing its mind and setting aside earlier judgements to meet the changing needs of society. However the notion of the Convention as a living instrument does not mean that the law can be developed on an arbitrary or piecemeal basis, with lower courts not accepting the decisions of higher courts. Accordingly the magistrate's court will still be bound by rulings of the Divisional Court (i.e. part of the High Court) and courts above that level, but the status of such decisions as well as their effect may now be argued whenever Convention rights are engaged.

Margin of appreciation

Not all the member countries of the Council of Europe view things from the same perspective. The doctrine of 'margin of appreciation' reflects the differences between the democratic traditions of the member states. The margin of appreciation has no role in national courts. Rather, it is a tool used by the Court of Human Rights to respect the lawful discretion which remains at national level to take action and be responsible for certain aspects of government. If there is a margin of appreciation in a set of circumstances it is for the European Court to identify it and *not* a national court.

The doctrine explained

Perhaps the best explanation for the doctrine is to follow the decision of the Court in *Handyside v. United Kingdom* (1976) 1 EHRR 737. In this case a publication called *The Little Red Schoolbook* was issued with children in mind. It included a chapter on sex. The books were seized by the police under the Obscene Publications Act 1959 and a forfeiture order obtained against the publishers. They in turn alleged a breach of Article 10 (freedom of expression), a qualified right.

The Court had to decide whether seizure of the books and the proceedings under the 1959 Act were necessary in a democratic society — that is to say whether the state was acting proportionally. The Court recognised that there existed a margin of appreciation in the case which justified the interference with Article 10. It stated:

> By reason of their direct and continuous contact with the vital forces of their countries, state authorities are in principle in a better position than the international judge to give an opinion on the exact nature of these requirements as well as on the necessity of a restriction or penalty intended to meet them . . . Nevertheless Article 10(2) does not give the contracting state an unlimited power of appreciation. The Court which is responsible for ensuring the observance of those states' engagements is empowered to give the final ruling on whether a restriction or penalty is reconcilable with freedom of expression as protected by Article 10. The domestic margin of appreciation thus goes hand in hand with a European supervision.

Under the doctrine the European Court has sometimes held back from making a finding on the issue of whether a particular domestic measure is proportional or justified under the Convention. Such cases do not really give guidance to national courts and there may well be decisions to be made domestically on points of Convention law where the

European Court has abstained from reaching a conclusion because of the margin of appreciation.

Positive obligation

The term 'positive obligation' has already been mentioned in *Chapter 1*. It refers to a series of implied or unwritten rights arising out of the express rights set out in the Convention. Positive obligations are sometimes difficult to identify and their existence seems to depend largely on the imagination of the Court in recognising them. Nevertheless they are an integral part of Convention law and an important source of rights. An example of a positive obligation arises from Article 2(1) (the right to life) and under which it is unlawful for a state to deprive someone of life except in certain conditions set out in Article 2(2) (*Chapter 3*).

Not only is there an obligation on the state to take no action leading to the loss of life but there is also a duty to take positive steps to preserve life. An issues for a magistrates' courts committee (MCC) to contemplate is that this duty may require a policy to be drawn up dealing with how, say, a violent or suicidal person is to be dealt with within a court building. As a public authority the MCC must act compatibly with the Convention and it is certainly responsible for the overall management of court premises. If a violent person were to be restrained by a court official or someone commits suicide in a court holding cell and there is no formal and effective policy or statement of practice in force for dealing with such eventualities then the MCC may be liable because Article 2 creates a positive obligation to take steps to ensure that life is preserved.

Proportionality

In the UK it is usually possible to challenge a judicial or official administrative decision on the basis that it is *unreasonable,* that is to say that no reasonable tribunal knowing all the facts and hearing all the arguments could have reached the same conclusion. In broad terms, this test of (ir)rationality is the standard applied by higher courts charged with conducting a judicial review of the decisions of lower courts and other public bodies. The test does not allow the higher court to substitute its own decision for the one under challenge, only to decide whether or not it was reasonable and in an appropriate case to quash the decision and/or send the case back to the original court to be reheard. In some cases the test has led to manifest injustice.

Under the Convention a test of *proportionality* is introduced into many areas of national law. In its colloquial form proportionality means not using a sledgehammer to crack a nut. It means doing no more than is necessary in order to achieve a particular end which itself is lawful and reasonable.

The Convention contains a number of qualified rights (see the examples in *Chapter 3*). The qualifications allow a state to interfere with the protected right in restricted circumstances. Usually there are three conditions which must be satisfied before a state can take advantage of a qualification. The interference must:

- be prescribed by law

- pursue one or more specified legitimate aims; and

- be no more than is necessary in a democratic society. The test of whether a measure is necessary in a democratic society is whether it is proportionate.

Example of a case involving 'proportionality'
The importance of the proportionality principle may become clearer after considering an example of everyday practice from the family proceedings court. A local authority may seek to remove a child from his parents on the basis that his welfare may suffer significant harm if he is allowed to remain in the parents' care. The removal of a child from his family clearly engages the rights of parents under Article 8(1) to a family life. The state may only interfere in the qualified circumstances set out in Article 8(2) (*Chapter 3*).

What the court will have to decide is whether there has been a breach of the parents' rights under Article 8, or put another way, whether the local authority can show that its interference meets the conditions in article 8(2). First, the interference is prescribed by law. The grounds for the removal of children are set out in the Children Act 1989. Second, protecting the child's welfare may well be one of the legitimate aims allowing interference under Article 8(2). But is the removal itself a proportionate response? This may be the most significant issue in the case for the magistrates to determine. The court would need to look at a range of issues. What is the nature of the harm suffered or likely to be suffered by the child? What alternatives are there to secure the same end? Could the local authority take a different course short of removing the child? For how long will the child be removed? What arrangements are there for contact between the child and his parents? Will the decision to remove the child be reviewed as time passes? All these matters go to the heart of whether the state's decision to interfere with the right to family life is proportional.

Proportionality not the same as reasonableness

The trap which it is easy to fall into is to ask whether the state's decision was 'reasonable'. Reasonableness and proportionality may not necessarily coincide and it is likely to be far harder for the state to satisfy a court that its interference with a right is proportional than it would be to satisfy the reasonableness test.

In *Dudgeon v. United Kingdom* (1981) 4 EHRR 149 a challenge was brought against a criminal law in Northern Ireland which made buggery between consenting gay adults an offence. The Court accepted that the law breached Article 8 in that it interfered with the right to private life. The Court looked at the government's reasons for upholding the law and accepted that the protection of vulnerable members of society was a legitimate aim. But in terms of whether the criminal law as it stood was proportional the Court said:

> It cannot be maintained in these circumstances that there is a pressing social need to make such acts criminal offences, there being no sufficient justification provided by the risk of harm to vulnerable sections of society requiring protection or by the effects on the public. On the issue of proportionality, the Court considers that such justifications as there are for retaining the law in force unamended are outweighed by the detrimental effects which the very existence of the legislative provisions in question can have on the life of a person of homosexual orientation like the applicant. Although members of the public who regard homosexuality as immoral may be shocked, offended or disturbed by the commission by others of private homosexual acts, this cannot on its own warrant the application of penal sanctions when it is consenting adults alone who are involved.

A further example may assist. Under section 13 Public Order Act 1986 a chief officer of police may apply to a local council for an order prohibiting all public processions on a given day where he or she believes that such a procession may result in serious disorder, damage or disruption. At present if the local authority grants such an order the only challenge available is by way of judicial review in the High Court where the applicant would have to persuade that court that no reasonable tribunal could have made the order—that it was a manifestly irrational decision to take.

When the Convention is in force the same order could be challenged in the High Court or in criminal proceedings in the magistrates' court arising out of non-compliance with the order. The approach however would be different. The applicant would need to show that a Convention right was engaged. Here the right to freedom of assembly under Article 11 is clearly engaged by an order banning assemblies and processions. Accordingly it would then fall to the local authority to persuade the court that:

- the prohibition was prescribed by law;
- it pursued a legitimate aim; and
- it was necessary in a democratic society.

This last condition means that the court would have to ask itself whether the measure was proportional. Was the interference with the rights under Article 11 at the lowest possible level necessary to secure the aim of the prohibition? Was a less intrusive but equally effective alternative remedy available?

The court in a traditional judicial review might well decide on these facts that the prohibition was one which fell into the range of prohibitions which a reasonable tribunal could make. The court might be of the view that, on reflection, the order was not one it would make itself but this would not prove fatal to the original order. The order would stand and the applicant would fail. However, applying the test of proportionality a court can explore other options and substitute its own view for that of the local authority irrespective of whether the original decision was reasonable or not. In this example it is possible that a less intrusive measure could have been adopted.

Rather than prohibiting all processions the local authority could have directed that the procession causing the police concern take a specific route, march only during certain times or be limited as to numbers in order to avoid disorder or disruption. The availability of these alternative measures goes to the heart of whether the original decision was proportional. The court might, on the full facts, find that the order made by the local authority was not a proportional response given the right to freedom of assembly. The order could be quashed by the High Court or the Convention right constitute a defence to a criminal charge.

Onus on the state

It seems highly likely that many courts will soon be occupied with resolving arguments founded upon the contention that a given interference with Convention rights is not proportional. In every case the court will need to conduct a balancing exercise weighing carefully the justifications against the standard that an interference must be necessary both as to means and ends and it will be for the state to prove that the measure is proportional.

STRUCTURED APPROACH

As indicated in *Chapter 1*, whenever a Convention right is engaged under the Human Rights Act 1998 the duty on the court is to interpret national legislation compatibly. This is a task requiring a structured approach. Fortunately, each of the rights in the Convention is drafted in very similar terms and accordingly the same approach can be used in each new situation where the court needs to deal with Convention issues. The structured approach involves identifying which right is engaged and asking a number of questions according to whether the right is absolute or the extent to which it is limited or qualified.

An example of a structured approach—what we have called a 'process map'—is contained in *Appendix II* (see pp.138-139). As with many of the concepts introduced by the Convention an example can also illustrate the point. The removal of children into care in an emergency clearly involves some interference with the right of the parents to family life under Article 8 (see *Chapter 3*). A court deciding whether to allow a local authority leave to remove children under an emergency protection order must have regard to Article 8(1) (which in these circumstances supports the right of the parents not to have their children removed). A Convention right is engaged. Article 8(2) allows the state, here the local authority, to interfere with the right to family life only under certain conditions. These are:

1. *That the basis of the interference is prescribed by law.* Here the court must look to see whether the grounds for the removal of children are set out with sufficient precision in national legislation. In the example the local authority is able to rely on the Children Act 1989 to satisfy the court that there is a lawful basis for intervention.

2. *That the interference pursues a legitimate aim.* The Convention prescribes a number of situations in which it is justifiable to interfere with the right to family life. The local authority may be able to rely on the protection of the rights of others—the children—where, e.g. they are at risk of suffering injury.

3. *That the measure is proportional.* Here the court must decide whether what the local authority intends to do is a proportionate response to the risk faced by the children if they do remain in the family. Could the local authority pursue a different and less intrusive course and still protect the children?

In the example the court has adopted the required structured approach. Not only is the decision likely to be compatible with the Convention but the approach provides an easy to use set of reasons for reaching a conclusion, whatever—on the facts of the particular case—that conclusion might be.

PURPOSIVE APPROACH

Traditionally the courts in the UK have interpreted and applied legislation literally—or at least in accordance with established legal understandings about the meanings of words in a given context. This is to say that, in general, the words of a statute are given their ordinary meaning and phrases are read as they appear unless there is some legal reason to do otherwise. This is a blunt description of interpretation in the UK and there are examples of creative thinking which do not strictly owe their origins to the literal approach, and which have nonetheless led to changes in law and procedure—and there are, to be fair, certain more sophisticated views and approaches to statutory interpretation, but it is generally accepted in the UK that it is not the task of the courts to supplement Acts of Parliament or to limit their effect—or even, in extreme instances, to make them 'workable'.

The Convention does not bear this type of strict interpretative scrutiny. It is as important for the rights *it does not expressly contain* as those it does and which are contained in the Articles. The task of the court—and this is a new task for English courts—is to look at the mischief which the right is aimed to prevent. The question to be asked is 'What is the purpose behind this provision?'. Thus, when a court interprets national legislation in situations where a Convention right is engaged it must look at the provision purposively. This may require giving generous consideration to the words, reading things into them in order to achieve the purpose of the law and not being bound by the precise and inflexible meaning of words on paper.

A note of caution
Again this does not mean that every court will be free to give effect to the law as it sees fit, regardless of the decisions of other higher courts. Nor does it mean that the law can be interpreted arbitrarily. The need for certainty in the law is in fact a right guaranteed by Article 6—and to some extent Article 7—of the Convention (*Chapter 3*). There remain clear rules of construction that will assist a court to interpret the law purposively without jeopardising the rule of law itself.

PROTOCOLS

Under the terms of membership of the Council of Europe the member states may from time to time agree to add to the rights contained in the Convention. Rather than revise the Convention each time this happens, a Protocol is drawn up setting out the additional rights. The First Protocol, e.g. provides for rights to the peaceful enjoyment of property, to education and to free elections. The 1998 Act allows the government to incorporate future protocols into national law by rules of Parliament. For example the Sixth Protocol provides for the abolition of the death penalty (which the UK, having signed, did not ratify until 1999). The rights contained in a Protocol carry the same weight as the rights set out in the Articles of the main body of the Convention. The Protocols are described in *Chapter 3*.

Chapter 2 Jargon, Jargon, Jargon

Some key points before proceeding to *Chapter 3*

This chapter emphasises the need:

- to be familiar with new words and phrases and to ensure that other people dealing with the court understand exactly what is under discussion

- to understand and apply key concepts. This facilitates the maintenance of a fair relationship between the state and the individual and serves to guarantee fair decision-making, including the right to a fair trial as required by Article 6

- to recognise that the Convention creates a series of conceptual tools and that these may often require a different approach to interpretation to that followed traditionally—including recognising 'positive obligations' and the need for a 'purposive approach'—both of which serve to enhance the protection of human rights

- to recognise that the principle of proportionality is particularly important in relation to qualified rights, but also generally in relation to Convention rights

- for a structured approach to decision-making which will allow the court to formulate sound reasons in support of its decision and to ensure that relevant concepts and principles have been correctly applied.

CHAPTER 3

Convention Rights

In this chapter we consider the various Articles of the European Convention on Human Rights as they will be incorporated into UK domestic law when the Human Rights Act 1998 takes effect.

A reminder and a cautionary note

From the outset it has to be appreciated that the Court has not always followed the literal meaning of the words of an Article. Reference to the judgements of the Court is essential in order to gain a true understanding of the full effect which an Article may have on court proceedings.

Also—as explained in *Chapter 2*—the relatively strict English doctrine of precedent is not one often followed by the Court, which regards the Convention as a living instrument to be interpreted in the light of present day conditions. Thus, generally speaking, rulings of the Court become less persuasive as time passes. This can be contrasted with the UK where, e.g. a decision of the House of Lords 20 or more years ago would need to be followed (or be distinguished as not applying to the facts of the present case) unless the law had been altered by Parliament in the meantime.

The Articles and Protocols incorporated by the 1998 Act are set out in full below with a short commentary attached to each (the Sixth Protocol is only summarised). Readers are reminded of the three categories of right described in *Chapter 2*, i.e. *absolute* rights, *limited* rights and *qualified* rights. After each article the status of the particular right is noted.

Article 2 *Right to Life*

Everyone's right to life shall be protected by law. No one shall be deprived of his life intentionally save in the execution of a sentence of a court following his conviction of a crime for which this penalty is provided by law

Deprivation of life shall not be regarded as inflicted in contravention of this article when it results from the use of force, which is no more than absolutely necessary

(a) in defence of any person from unlawful violence;
(b) in order to effect a lawful arrest or to prevent the escape of a person lawfully detained;
(c) in action lawfully taken for the purpose of quelling a riot or insurrection.

This is a *limited* right which has been described by the Court as 'one of the most fundamental provisions in the Convention'. It may be rare for the scope of this article to fall for consideration in a magistrates' court (but see the comments about the positive obligations of public authorities in this regard mentioned in *Chapter 2*).

Article 3 *Prohibition of torture*

No one shall be subjected to torture or to inhuman or degrading treatment or punishment

This is an *absolute* right. For Article 3 to become relevant the conduct complained of must 'attain a minimum level of severity' (*Ireland v. UK* (1978) 2 EHRR 25). In that case guidelines were given to help assess whether the conduct reaches this required level. The guidelines define the three separate categories of prohibited treatment as follows:

- *Torture*
  Deliberate inhuman treatment causing very serious and cruel suffering.

- *Inhuman treatment/punishment*
  Treatment/punishment that causes intense physical and mental suffering.

- *Degrading treatment/punishment*
  Treatment/punishment that arouses in the victim a feeling of fear, anguish and inferiority capable of humiliating and debasing the victim and possibly breaking his or her physical or moral resistance.

The following are examples of where Article 3 might need to be considered in magistrates' courts:

- under sections 3(6) and 6 of the Immigration Act 1971 a court can recommend for deportation anyone over the age of 17 (not having a right of abode in this country), who is convicted of an offence which carries imprisonment. After the 1998 Act is in force a defendant might argue that his or her rights under Article 3 would be breached if a recommendation for deportation was made where it is likely that if the defendant was deported he or she would be subject to treatment prohibited by that Article.

- possibly in relation to breaches of Article 3 by the police leading to the exclusion of evidence: this is considered further in *Chapter 6*.

- magistrates are frequently asked to rule on whether a defendant who is in custody can be handcuffed when brought into court. Previous decisions of the Commission have held that this does not amount to a breach of Article 3. Commentators on recent case law emanating from Strasbourg have noted, however, an increased sensitivity to the appearance of fairness. Thus in a case decided in 1997 the Commission held that *unnecessary* handcuffing of a person arrested and brought before a court *was* degrading treatment in breach of Article 3 (*Kaj Ranninen v. Finland* (1997) EHRR 176). However, late in 1999 the Court overruled this decision.

Article 4 *Prohibition of slavery and forced labour*

(1) No one shall be held in slavery or servitude.

(2) No one shall be required to perform forced or compulsory labour.

(3) For the purpose of this article the term 'forced or compulsory labour' shall not include:
  - (a) any work required to be done in the ordinary course of detention imposed according to the provisions of Article 5 of this Convention or during conditional release from such detention;
  - (b) any service of a military character or, in case of conscientious objectors in countries where they are recognised, service exacted instead of compulsory military service;
  - (c) any service exacted in case of emergency or calamity threatening the life or well-being of the community;
  - (d) any work or service which forms part of normal civic obligations.

Article 4(1) contains an *absolute* right and Article 4(2) a *limited* right. Peacetime derogation is possible from Article 4(2) but the UK has not entered any derogations. Generally speaking, this Article may be of small relevance in the magistrates' court with the possible exception of the abolition of the requirement for consent to certain community sentences. The removal of the need for consent by section 38 Crime (Sentences) Act 1997 would seem, at present, to leave open the question of whether domestic law contravenes Article 4(2). The situation will exist whereby someone could be forced without consent to perform compulsory labour or suffer the legal consequences. The authors suggest that it might be prudent for the time being and until the Court provides guidance for magistrates to ask for consent once the 1998 Act is in force, and to ensure that consent is recorded—because arguments based on Article 4(2) might well be raised in later 'breach' proceedings. The Article may also be relevant in analogous situations in the youth court (see *Chapter 11*).

Article 5 *Right to liberty and security*

(1) Everyone has the right to liberty and security of person. No one shall be deprived of his liberty save in the following cases and in accordance with a procedure prescribed by law:

(a) the lawful detention of a person after conviction by a competent court;

(b) the lawful arrest or detention of a person for non–compliance with the lawful order of a court or in order to secure the fulfillment of any obligation prescribed by law;

(c) the lawful arrest or detention of a person effected for the purpose of bringing him before the competent legal authority on reasonable suspicion of having committed an offence or when it is reasonably considered necessary to prevent his committing an offence or fleeing after having done so;

(d) the detention of a minor by lawful order for the purpose of educational supervision or his lawful detention for the purpose of bringing him before the competent legal authority;

(e) the lawful detention of persons for the spreading of infectious diseases, of persons of unsound mind, alcoholics or drug addicts

(f) the lawful arrest or detention of a person to prevent his effecting an unauthorised entry into the country or of a person against whom action is being taken with a view to deportation or extradition.

(2) Everyone who is arrested shall be informed promptly, in a language, which he understands, of the reasons for his arrest and of any charge against him.

(3) Everyone arrested or detained in accordance with paragraph 1(c) of this article shall be brought before a judge or other officer authorised by law exercise judicial power and shall be entitled to trial within a reasonable time or to release pending trial. Release may be conditioned by guarantees to appear for trial.

(4) Everyone who is deprived of his liberty by arrest or detention shall be entitled to take proceedings by which the lawfulness of his detention shall be decided speedily by a court and his release ordered if the detention is not lawful.

(5) Everyone who has been the victim of arrest or detention in contravention of the provisions of this article shall have an exercisable right to compensation

This is a *limited* right and clearly of considerable relevance to the work of the magistrates' courts. The protection given by the Article can be summarised:

• No one can be deprived of his or her liberty except in accordance with a procedure prescribed by law.

- The only grounds upon which someone may be deprived of their liberty are set out in Article 5(1)(a) to (f) and *this list is exhaustive,* i.e. there is no other lawful basis for depriving someone of their liberty.

- Anyone subject to detention must be able to challenge the legality of that detention.

- If it is determined that someone has been detained in violation of this Article, he or she has an enforceable right to compensation.

The right to liberty: UK derogation
The UK has entered a derogation in respect of pre-trial detention. The background to this was the case of *Brogan and Others v. UK* (1988) 11 EHRR 117 where the Court held that the detention of the applicants under the Prevention of Terrorism (Temporary Provisions) Act 1984 for more than four days was a breach of Article 5(3). The derogation presently entered allows detention for up to seven days and this was upheld by the Court in *Brannigan and McBride v. UK* (1993) 17 EHRR 539 (the legality of derogations can be scrutinised by the Court of Human Rights).

Areas where the UK complies with the right to liberty
There are areas of domestic law which appear to be compliant with Article 5. For example the provisions of the Police and Criminal Evidence Act 1984 (PACE) and the Codes of Practice thereunder regarding the detention and treatment of suspects in accordance with the Codes seem to meet the requirements of Article 5(2) to (4). Similarly the Prosecution of Offences (Custody Time Limits) Regulations 1987 appear to cover the requirement in Article 5(3) of entitlement to trial within a reasonable time or to be released pending that trial.

Contentious areas
There remain a number of situations where magistrates may face Convention-based arguments. For example, under section 60 Criminal Justice and Public Order Act 1994 a senior police officer may authorise other officers to stop and search people and vehicles in an area for offensive weapons where he or she believes that serious violence may occur. By virtue of section 60(5) of that Act there is no requirement for a police officer to have a reasonable suspicion when searching. Failure to stop is an imprisonable offence. The only relevant ground under Article 5 to justify someone's loss of liberty in these circumstances would, arguably, be that set out in Article 5(1)(c)—but this would require the officer to have a reasonable suspicion.

The domestic legislation appears therefore to be incompatible with the Convention and under section 3 of the 1998 Act the court would need to decide whether it was possible to read into section 60(5) those words which would give effect to the Convention, that is to say a requirement on the officer to have a reasonable suspicion. If it were not possible to do so the court's duty would be to follow the words of the statute. This could readily lead to the conviction of a defendant despite the breach of his rights under the Convention.

In such a case would the court feel constrained—as some commentators suggest—to impose nothing more severe than an absolute discharge? Or should the court accept that the law must be enforced as it stands and not as it should be—and go on to pass the 'appropriate' sentence? Such dilemmas are likely to become 'meat and drink' once the 1998 Act is in force.

A further area of difficulty arising under Article 5 is in the family proceedings court which at present hears applications by local authorities under section 25 Children Act 1989 for an authority to place children accommodated by them in secure accommodation. Such orders restricting a child or young person's liberty are *prima facie* in breach of Article 5. The criteria in domestic legislation may result in a child with no criminal involvement being held in secure accommodation. It is arguable that such an order would be incompatible with any of the exceptions to the right to liberty set out in Article 5. The coming into force of the Human Rights Act 1998 may sound the death knell for such applications to the family proceedings court although stronger arguments can be found in support of the power to make such orders in the course of criminal proceedings. In most cases in family proceedings the local authority's application is likely to be based on the risk of absconding and injury to the child and in *Re M (a minor) (Secure Accommodation Order)* (1995) 3 All ER 407 the Court of Appeal held that if the criteria were established the court must make the order. This would seem to be a case where justices might have to consider disregarding earlier UK case law and decline to make an order.

Article 6 *Right to a fair trial*

(1) In the determination of his civil rights and obligations or of any criminal charge against him, everyone is entitled to a fair and public hearing within a reasonable time by an independent and impartial tribunal established by law. Judgement shall be pronounced publicly but the press and public may be excluded from all or part of the trial in the interests of morals, public order or national security in a democratic society, where the interests of juveniles or the protection of the private life of the parties so require, or to

the extent strictly necessary in the opinion of the court in special circumstances where publicity would prejudice the interest of justice.

(2) Everyone charged with a criminal offence shall be presumed innocent until proved guilty according to law.

(3) Everyone charged with a criminal offence has the following minimum rights:
  (a) to be informed promptly, in a language he understands and in detail, of the nature and cause of the accusation against him;
  (b) to have adequate time and facilities for the preparation of his defence;
  (c) to defend himself in person or though legal assistance of his own choosing or, if he has not sufficient means to pay for legal assistance, to be given it free when the interest of justice so require;
  (d) to examine or have examined witnesses against him and to obtain the attendance and examination of witnesses on his behalf under the same conditions as witnesses against him;
  (e) to have the free assistance of an interpreter if he cannot understand or speak the language used in court.

Article 6 contains a range of *absolute* and *limited* rights which will clearly have a great bearing on the conduct of proceedings in all courts of law. In practice, there have been more applications to Strasbourg concerning Article 6 than with regard to any other Article in the Convention.

No restrictive interpretation
The first point to emphasise is that 'there can be no justification for interpreting Article 6(1) of the Convention restrictively' (*Moreira de Azevedo v. Portugal* (1990) 13 EHRR 721).

Extra protection in criminal proceedings
Article 6(1) covers trials 'determining civil rights and obligations' (e.g. the issue of contact between a parent and child, care proceedings) as well as criminal charges. However Article 6(2) and (3) give specific *further rights* when someone is facing a criminal charge. It is important therefore to determine when a charge is 'criminal'. In *Engel v. Netherlands* (1976) 1 EHRR 644 the court made clear that 'criminal charge' is an autonomous concept. In other words, the Strasbourg institutions will decide for themselves whether particular proceedings involve the determination of such a charge within the meaning of Article 6. For further discussion of this recurring aspect see particularly *Chapters 5* and *8*.

Equality of arms and Article 6
The Court in *Neumesiter v. Austria* (1979 to 1980) 1 EHRR 91 developed the concept known as *equality of arms* (*Chapter 2*). This means that 'each

party must be afforded a reasonable opportunity to present his or her case—including his evidence under conditions that do not place him at a substantial disadvantage vis–à–vis his opponent'. This principle might be particularly relevant when considering the law on advance disclosure and is discussed again in *Chapter 5.*

Article 7 *No punishment without law*

(1) No one shall be held guilty of any criminal offence on account of any act or omission, which did not constitute a criminal offence under national or international law at the time when it was committed. Nor shall a heavier penalty be imposed than the one that was applicable at the time the criminal offence was committed.

(2) This article shall not prejudice the trial and punishment of any person for any act or omission, which, at the time when it was committed, was criminal according to the general principles of law, recognised by civilised nations.

This is an *absolute* right which may be prayed in aid of arguments that a provision of the criminal law is 'vague' or 'uncertain'. That aspect apart, it is unusual for Parliament to impose retrospective penalties, there being a domestic legal presumption against retro-activity in relation to criminal matters. However, current changes in the law concerning sex offenders will need to be looked at carefully. For example the Criminal Evidence (Amendment) Act 1997 allows the police to take samples for DNA profiling of those convicted of offences before that Act came into force. Is this a retrospective 'penalty' in breach of Article 7? It is far from clear. The same might be argued in respect of 'three strikes' mandatory sentences under the Crime (Sentences) Act 1997 in so far as any such offences in the sequence occurred before that Act—or, indeed, whenever there is a transition to a regime which involves enhanced penalties whether for repeat convictions or where just related to a single offence.

Article 7 in practice
Two European Court cases involving the UK demonstrate what is involved and give some background as to how Article 7 has been interpreted:

- in *Welch v United Kingdom* (1995) 20 EHRR 247 the applicant was arrested on drug charges in November 1986. In January 1987, the law was changed relating to the seizure of any proceeds gained as a result of drug trafficking. The applicant submitted that if the new law applied to him it would constitute retrospective legislation and offend Article 7. The UK argued that the new law did not involve any penalties. The Court however ruled that the retrospective application of the confiscation order was a penalty and offended Article 7. They found that the applicant faced more 'far reaching detriment' as a result of the government seizure than he would have done at the time he committed the offences in question.

- however, in *SW and CR v. UK* (1996) 21 EHRR 363 it was held that the change in the law making rape within marriage a crime was sufficiently foreseeable to mean that Article 7 was not violated when a husband was convicted of raping his wife.

Article 8 *Right to respect for private and family life*

(1) Everyone has the right to respect for his private and family life, his home and his correspondence.

(2) There shall be no interference by a public authority with the exercise of this right except such as is in accordance with the law and is necessary in a democratic society and in the interests of national security, public safety or the economic well-being of the country, for the prevention of disorder or crime, for the protection of health and morals, or for the protection of the rights and freedoms of others.

This is a *qualified* right of huge importance. Many academic commentators feel that our domestic law is due for some considerable development in this area when the Human Rights Act 1998 is implemented. Most Strasbourg case law is concerned with the definition of the terms 'private life', 'family life', 'home' and 'correspondence'. The Court has held that the 'essential object of Article 8 is to protect the individual against arbitrary action by public authorities'.

Positive and negative obligations
Article 8 imposes both positive and negative obligations on states. The positive obligation to ensure respect for the rights given in this Article impose an obligation to provide for effective respect for private life, e.g. by ensuring that domestic law provides for this. On the negative side, if the state is to interfere with someone's private and family life, home or correspondence the interference must be justified by one of the exceptions detailed in Article 8(2) and must be the minimum necessary to achieve that specific, legitimate aim. Only those exceptions are allowed. Once the state has identified a legitimate objective prescribed by law, the Court focuses on proportionality. It will ask whether the interference serves 'a pressing social need'.

The effect of Article 8 on family proceedings courts is considered further in *Chapter 6.*

Search warrants

Beyond the family court an obvious case where this Article may affect the work of magistrates is in relation to applications for search warrants. The relevant UK law (principally contained in the Police and Criminal Evidence 1984) contains safeguards that should comply with Article 8. However magistrates will need to continue to be meticulous when dealing with such applications. If valid reasons do not exist or are not properly recorded, challenges under the Convention might be hard to defend. The practice, hopefully rare, of police officers approaching magistrates directly and individually rather than through the court administration should cease.

Contrasting findings

Article 8 may also have an impact in criminal proceedings. Two contrasting examples illustrate how interpretation of the protection given to private life could be relevant in criminal courts. In *Sutherland v. UK* (1998) Vol. 1 EHRLR 117 the Commission took the view that the different ages of consent as between heterosexuals and homosexuals breached Articles 8 and 14 (prohibition of discrimination). In *Laskey, Jaggard and Brown v. United Kingdom* (1997) 24 EHRR 39 the Court considered that consensual sado-masochism resulting in convictions for assault and wounding did not amount to a breach of Article 8.

Article 9 *Freedom of thought, conscience and religion*

(1) Everyone has the right to freedom of thought, conscience and religion; this right includes freedom to change his religion or belief and freedom either alone or in community with others and in public or private, to manifest his religion or belief, in worship, teaching, practice and observance.

(2) Freedom to manifest one's religion or beliefs shall be subject only to such limitations as are prescribed by law and are necessary in a democratic society in the interests of public safety, for the protection of public order, health or morals, or for the protection of the rights and freedoms of others.

The right to hold religious beliefs is *absolute,* whereas the right to manifest them may be *limited* under Article 9(2).

Guidance on Article 9

There is little case law from the Court which seems relevant to the work of the courts. An example of the sort of situation where applications have been made alleging breach of Article 9 is *Stedman v. UK* (1997) 23 EHRLR 168. This application was by a Christian alleging breach by having to work on Sundays. The Court held that a state could be required to protect an employee from a private company but said there was no need to do so in that particular case: the applicant had been dismissed for failing to agree to work certain hours, not for her religious beliefs. She had been free to resign. This approach is perhaps more restrictive than the one which is likely to be followed in the UK.

An example of relevance to magistrates' courts illustrates the potential importance of Article 9. Consider the position if a local authority refused planning permission for the construction of a Sikh temple citing as its reason the likely adverse public reaction to such a development. The local authority may itself be liable in damages for its refusal which may be regarded as a breach of Article 9. A discussion of the local authority's potential civil liability falls outside the scope of this book, but what if, in such a case, the temple was built without planning permission and after taking certain enforcement steps against the owners the local authority brought a prosecution under the Town and Country Planning Act 1971? Here the temple owners might be able to rely on Article 9 as a defence, in that the local authority would have to show that its interference with the right of local Sikhs to manifest their religious beliefs by constructing a temple was both lawful and proportionate. Given that Article 14, discussed later provides for equality of Convention rights without discrimination, this combination of Convention rights might be sufficient to defeat the local authority's case.

Article 10 *Freedom of expression*

(1) Everyone has the right to freedom of expression. This right shall include freedom to hold opinions and to receive and impart information and ideas without interference by public authority and regardless of frontiers. This article shall not prevent States from requiring the licensing of broadcasting, television or cinema enterprises.

(2) The exercise of these freedoms, since it carries duties and responsibilities, may be subject to such formalities, conditions, restrictions or penalties as are prescribed by law and are necessary in a democratic society, in the interests of national security, territorial integrity, or public safety, for the prevention of disorder or crime, for the protection of health and morals, for the protection of the reputation or rights of others, for preventing the disclosure of information received in confidence, or for maintaining the authority and impartiality of the judiciary.

This is a *qualified* right. The concept of 'freedom of expression' was defined in *Handyside v. UK* (1976) 1 EHRR 737:

> Freedom of expression constitutes one of the essential foundations of a [democratic] society, one of its basic conditions for progress and for the development of every man. Subject to paragraph 2 of Article 10, it is applicable not only to 'information' or 'ideas' that are favourably received and regarded as inoffensive but also to those that offend, shock or disturb the state or any sector of the population. Such are the demands of pluralism, tolerance and broadmindedness without which there is no democratic society.

It can be seen that Article 10(2) is longer and contains more potential restrictions than other Articles, making the fine line and the balance between this right and the rights and freedoms of others difficult to draw. Also, this right can conflict with competing social interests such as the right to a fair trial (Article 6), and the rights of other people to freedom of thought, conscience and religion (Article 9).

Protection of Article 10 rights by the European Court of Human Rights
There is a great deal of case law on this Article. It would appear that the Court in practice gives considerable protection to political and journalistic expression. In any case where Article 10(1) is engaged, particular attention needs to be paid to whether the restriction concerned has been prescribed by law and is proportional in accordance with Article 10(2). An example of this can be seen in *Goodwin v. UK* (1996) 22 EHRR 469 where a journalist had been fined for contempt of court for refusing to disclose his 'sources'. The Court found a *prima facie* breach of Article 10(1)—but in interpreting Article 10(2) found that the UK court's decision was 'prescribed by law' and 'pursued a legitimate aim'. Nonetheless it found that the fine was disproportionate in the circumstances.

Another example showing how the criminal law may be affected is *Bowman v. UK* (1998) 26 EHRR. The applicant was convicted under section 75 Representation of the People Act 1983 which makes it an offence for an unauthorised person to incur more than £5 expenditure distributing leaflets etc. during an election period with a view to securing the election of a candidate. The applicant was a member of an anti-abortion campaign and sent leaflets to electors highlighting the views of candidates on abortion. The Court found that Article 10 was breached in that the effect of section 75 was effectively to prevent this group from putting over to the electorate their views.

In the magistrates' court, the most common instances where Article 10 might be relevant will be prosecutions arising from political demonstrations. A sound understanding of the 'balancing act' required by Article 10(2) will be needed.

Article 11 *Freedom of assembly and association*

(1) Everyone has the right to freedom of peaceful assembly and to freedom of association with others, including the right to form and to join trade unions for the protection of his interests.

(2) No restrictions shall be placed on the exercise of these rights other than such as are prescribed by law and are necessary in a democratic society in the interest of national security or public safety, for the prevention of disorder or crime, for the protection of health or morals or for the protection of the rights and freedoms of others. This article shall not prevent the imposition of lawful restrictions on the exercise of these rights by members of the armed forces, of the police or of the administration of the State

This is a *qualified* right which may again result in courts having to make difficult decisions balancing the exercise of the right against other rights in the Convention.

A positive obligation under Article 11
Case law has created a positive obligation for authorities to protect the exercise of the rights contained in the Article.

Genuine, effective freedom of peaceful assembly cannot " be reduced to a mere duty on the part of the State not to interfere: a purely negative conception would not be compatible with the object and purpose of Article 11". Article 11 sometimes requires positive measures to be taken, even in the sphere of relations between individuals, if need be (*Plattform Ärzte für das Leben v. Austria* (1988) 13 EHRR 204)

How far does this positive obligation extend? It is difficult to predict the scope of the duty but an example may help. Consider a peaceful demonstration by a group of hunt protesters which on a number of occasions is disrupted and harassed by a rival group in support of hunting. The alleged harassment is so intense that it leads to prosecutions under the Protection from Harassment Act 1997. Pursuant to the 1997 Act magistrates' courts can, on conviction, consider whether to make a retraining order (prohibiting specified behaviour in future). In this case, just prosecuting the offenders may not be enough. The state must take action to prevent the peaceful demonstration from being disrupted in the future. The positive obligation may also extend so as to inform magistrates how they should exercise their discretion. In this example the positive obligation to protect the rights under Article 11 may *require* the court to make a restraining order where it might otherwise have declined to do so.

In relation to freedom of assembly, the right given by Article 11 only applies to peaceful gatherings and does not encompass 'a demonstration where the organizers and participants have violent intentions which result in public disorder' (*G v. Federal Republic of Germany* (1989) 69 DR 256). The right to freedom of association may well arise in relation to public order, even if existing case law is mainly concerned with trade union law and somewhat removed from the criminal courts. Also, bail conditions may prohibit association with certain people when this right may fall to be considered: see, generally, *Chapter 5.*

Likelihood of Article 11 defences

When the Human Rights Act 1998 is implemented it is likely that many defences will be put forward based upon Article 11. They may have a chance of success if national law is found to be insufficiently clear or restrictions imposed, perhaps by the police on marches etc., are not proportionate or necessary in a democratic society: see the further discussion of such matters in *Chapter 2* (p.28).

Article 12 *Right to marry*

> Men and women of marriageable age have the right to marry and to found a family, according to the national laws governing the exercise of this right.

This *limited* right carries no exception clause and gives the state wide scope to regulate the exercise of the right. Article 12 is far less wide-ranging than Article 8 which protects family life. It does not give a right to found a family outside marriage and only applies to biologically opposite sexes. An example of the wide powers given to the state is *Johnson v Ireland* (1987) 9 EHRR 203 where it was held that there was no violation of Article 12 if a state prohibits a divorcee from re-marrying.

Article 13 *Right to an effective remedy*

> Everyone whose rights and freedoms as set forth in the convention are violated shall have an effective remedy before a national authority notwithstanding that the violation has been committed by persons acting in an official capacity.

This Article giving a right to a remedy if Convention rights are broken has not been directly incorporated in the UK (the reason why it is omitted from the schedule to the Human Rights Act 1998), as the government believes the 1998 Act provides effective remedies. In addition, the Act tries to balance Parliamentary sovereignty and the power of the courts to apply the rights set out in the Convention and give effective remedies. The power of the higher courts under section 4 of the 1998 Act to make declarations of incompatibility and the provisions relating to remedial action in Parliament found in sections 10 to 12 are all part of a framework to achieve this balance. To have incorporated Article 13 directly into UK law could, according to one school of thought, have allowed courts to overturn primary legislation.

Article 14 *Prohibition of discrimination*

The enjoyment of the rights and freedoms set forth in this Convention shall be secured without discrimination on any ground such as sex, race, colour, language, religion, political or other opinion, national or social origin, association with a national minority, property, birth or other status.

We are already used to the idea of the law protecting minorities, e.g. the Race Relations Act 1976 and 'racially aggravated' sentencing provisions. It is also the case that discrimination is unlawful pursuant to the rules of natural justice. But a clear understanding of the effect of this Article is difficult to find when analysing Strasbourg case law. A number of comments can be made:

- Article 14 does not create an independent right; it only operates to prevent discrimination in the context of other Convention rights.

- the Article is, however, broader than domestic anti-discriminatory laws and the phrase 'or other status' has been widely interpreted.

- not all forms of differentiation will breach Article 14: it is only different treatment of people placed in 'an analogous situation' which falls within its scope. Therefore the Court has held that the different treatment of gay and heterosexual relationships is not discriminatory when dealing with a claim under Article 8 concerning the sharing of the parental role (*Kerkhoven v. Netherlands*, Application No.15666/89, 19 May 1992). This case is perhaps a good example of how the Court will, as already indicated, construe Article 14 only in the context of other Convention rights. Discrimination of this type when considering the rights given under Article 6 relating to people accused of criminal offences would probably breach Article 14—as, in the context of Article 6, the court would be comparing people in 'an analogous situation'.

When the 1998 Act is implemented one possible example of Article 14 being relevant in proceedings in a magistrates' court would be if a police force exercises its stop and search powers in a way which disproportionately affects people from ethnic minorities. Then criminal proceedings may well involve issues arising from both Article 10 (freedom of expression) and Article 14.

Article 16 *Restrictions on political activity of aliens*

Nothing in Articles 10, 11 and 14 shall be regarded as preventing the High Contracting Parties [the States] from imposing restrictions on the political activities of aliens.

Recent cases have suggested that this provision may be somewhat outdated. When considering an application under Article 10 (freedom of expression) and Article 11 (freedom of assembly and association) where Article 16 is raised as a 'defence' the words of paragraph 2 of each of those articles would need to be examined and any restrictions on the activities of aliens would have to be shown to serve a legitimate aim and to be proportionate (*Piermont v. France* (1995) EHRR 301).

Since the Single European Act—better known as the Maastrict Treaty—citizens of the European Union can no longer be regarded as aliens within Europe.

Article 17 *Prohibition of abuse of rights*

Nothing in this Convention may be interpreted as implying for any State, group or person any right to engage in any activity or perform any act aimed at the destruction of any rights and freedoms set forth herein or at their limitation to a greater extent than is provided for in the Convention.

An obvious but important provision.

Article 18 *Limitation on use of restriction of rights*

The restrictions permitted under this Convention to the said rights and freedoms shall not be applied for any purpose other than those for which they have been prescribed.

This Article could perhaps be regarded as superfluous but it does serve to emphasise the numerous instances above of Articles which are subject to restrictions. The task in practice will be to decide what is the real objective behind the imposition of any restriction of a right.

PROTOCOLS

As explained in *Chapters 1* and *2*, the Convention can be adapted and extended by way of what are termed 'Protocols'. The 1998 Act incorporates two existing protocols, the first and sixth:

The First Protocol: **Article 1** Protection of property

> Every natural or legal person is entitled to the peaceful enjoyment of his possessions. No one shall be deprived of his possessions except in the public interest and subject to the conditions provided for by law and by general principles of international law.
>
> The preceding provisions shall not, however, in any way impair the right of a State to enforce such laws as it deems necessary to control the use of property in accordance with the general interest or to secure the payment of taxes or other contributions or penalties.

This is perhaps one of the more controversial rights under the Convention. Some people would argue that these rights are really economic rights rather than human rights. Article 1 of the First Protocol is highly qualified and Strasbourg in interpreting it has allowed states a wide 'margin of appreciation'. The Court has analysed this Article and broken it down into three parts:

- the principle of peaceful enjoyment

- the prohibition against deprivation of possession, unless certain conditions are complied with; and

- the right of the state to control the use of property by enforcing such laws as it deems necessary.

In determining the issues under the second limb of Article 1, the level of permissible interference, the Court applies the 'fair balance' test. Any interference must achieve a fair balance between the general interests of the community and the protection of the individual's rights. In assessing whether a fair balance has been achieved it has insisted that domestic law provide a clear procedure for determining the issue and that there should be an effective remedy to deal with any disputes. The question of compensating an individual for a breach of this Article is also an issue to be considered. But in exceptional circumstances inadequate compensation may not breach this Article if the state has legitimate public grounds for enacting the law concerned. A good example of the way the law operates is the case of *James v. UK* (1986) 8 EHRR 123 which involved the compulsory transfer of residential properties in London under the Leasehold Reform Act 1967 (which was designed to protect long term tenants' moral entitlement to their properties). The property landowners complained that the compulsory nature and calculation of the price of the transfers violated Article 1. The Court held that the transfer was a legitimate means of promoting the public interest, even where the community at large had no direct enjoyment of the property taken. The elimination of social injustice by leasehold reform was within the states' margin of appreciation. Legitimate objectives of public interest may call for reimbursement at less then full value.

The enforcement of a fine for a minor offence, such as not having a TV licence, by way of automatic distress or imprisonment (see *Chapter 8*) may arguably be a disproportionate response and an interference with the rights set out in this Article.

Magistrates are most likely to deal with the First Protocol, Article 1 when considering the third limb. Controls on the use of property, which have been held not to violate this article include laws requiring positive action to be taken by property owners such as environmental laws requiring them to plant trees. Negative laws relating to property rights include planning controls, the breach of which could give rise to criminal proceedings before magistrates.

Another example of domestic laws which have been considered and approved by the Court and which involve 'control on the use of property' are the forfeiture rules in the Obscene Publications Act 1956. These were examined in *Handyside v. UK* (1976) 1 EHRR 737 where the Court found there had been no violation where books adjudged to be obscene were seized and destroyed by the state (see also *Chapter 2*).

The law concerning occupation orders (i.e. regulating occupation of the family home) under the Family Law Act 1996 may also attract arguments under this Article. Whilst the overall scheme of things under the FLA 1996 appears to be compatible with the Convention the court will need to carefully examine the circumstances in which any application is allowed to proceed 'without notice' and upon the duration of such an order which—to be proportionate—should generally be for the shortest possible time.

The First Protocol: **Article 2** *Right to Education*

No person shall be denied the right to education. In the exercise of any functions which it assumes in relation to education and to teaching, the State shall respect the right of parents to ensure such education and teaching in conformity with their own religious and philosophical convictions.

The UK has formally lodged a reservation in respect of this Article to the extent that 'the principle affirmed in the second sentence of Article 2 is accepted by the UK only in so far as it is compatible with the provision of efficient instruction and training, and the avoidance of unreasonable public expenditure'.

Article 2 covers both primary and secondary education. A state may limit tertiary education to those who will benefit from it (*X v. UK* DR 228 (1980)). The state may require parents to send their children to school or to educate them adequately at home (*Family H v. UK* 37 DR (1984)). The lawfulness of local education authorities bringing applications for supervision orders would appear to be compatible with the Article.

The second sentence of Article 2 prevents the state using the education system to indoctrinate pupils. Parents have the right to have their religious and philosophical convictions respected.

In *Campbell and Cosans v. UK* (1982) 4 EHRR 292 two parents challenged the existence of corporal punishment in state schools on the basis that it was contrary to their philosophical beliefs. Their complaint was upheld; their views on corporal punishment could be classified as 'philosophical convictions'. Such convictions were worthy of respect in a democratic society, were not incompatible with human dignity and did not conflict with the fundamental right of the child to education. The School Standards and Framework Act 1998 now outlaws corporal punishment.

There seem to be few, if any, obvious examples where an interpretation of this Article will have to be considered by magistrates, particularly in view of the reservation by the UK. However the facility for state education may arise, e.g. in the family proceedings court or in prosecutions for failing to ensure the attendance of a child at school (something that the present government has announced that it intends to 'toughen up' on) or where such conviction could lead to the making of a parenting order under the Crime and Disorder Act 1998 (see *Chapter 11*).

The First Protocol: **Article 3** *Free elections*

The High Contracting Parties [States] undertake to hold free elections at reasonable intervals by secret ballot, under conditions which will ensure the free expression of the opinion of the people in the choice of the legislature.

Perhaps only in the unlikeliest of situations would this be a right for magistrates to interpret—but this is not inconceivable, say, in relation to electoral expenses or fraud.

The Sixth Protocol

In 1999, the UK finally ratified the sixth protocol to the European Convention on Human Rights which effectively outlaws the death penalty. It was abolished for all but a few obscure crimes under the Murder (Abolition of Death Penalty Act) 1965 and it can now only be revived in time of war or imminent threat of war.

Chapter 3: Convention Rights

Some key points before proceeding in the rest of this book to look at the practical application of the Convention under the Human Rights Act 1998 and in relation to various aspects of court work. This chapter:

- emphasises the importance of understanding the various categories of rights under the Convention—*absolute, limited* and *qualified*—and their effect on the balance of power between states and individuals

- indicates why it is important:
  —to be able to identify the rights and freedoms contained in the Convention which are capable of protection by a court; and
  —to understand the way in which the Court in Strasbourg has approached the interpretation of different rights in the various Articles and Protocols

- is also about courts and public authorities helping to create a better society based on the rule of law, equality, certainty and accessibility.

Chapter 4

Human Rights in Practice

The long title of the Human Rights Act 1998[1] states that it is an Act 'to give further effect to rights and freedoms guaranteed under the European Convention on Human Rights'. This chapter looks at the legal and judicial mechanisms via which these rights and freedoms will be delivered in practice.

Section 2(1)

In stating the key duty of a court section 2(1) of the 1998 Act provides:

> A court or tribunal determining a question that has arisen in connection with a Convention right must take into account any -
> (a) judgement, decision, declaration or advisory opinion of the European Court of Human Rights,
> (b) opinion of the Commission given in a report adopted under Article 31 of the Convention,
> (c) decision of the Commission in connection with Article 26 or 27(2) of the Convention, or
> (d) decision of the Committee of Ministers taken under Article 46 of the Convention
> whenever made or given, so far as, in the opinion of the court or tribunal, it is relevant to the proceedings in which the question has arisen.

A magistrates' court is a court of inferior jurisdiction and its jurisdiction and procedures are contained in statute, principally the Magistrates' Courts Act 1980 and Justices of the Peace Act 1979 (and associated rules). In addition, all criminal or civil powers in that court arise under the operation of legislation emanating from Parliament, i.e. either:

- *primary* legislation (Acts of Parliament); or

- *subordinate* legislation made, e.g. by a minister of state acting under the authority of an Act of Parliament (statutory instruments, often called 'secondary legislation', 'rules' or 'regulations').

These courts are further governed by rulings, directions and guidance provided by the higher courts which —under UK law—bind lower courts according to established rules of precedent.

---

[1] The main provisions of the Human Rights Act 1998 are reproduced in *Appendix I* to this work. Schedule 1 to the Act which contains the Articles and Protocols is not reproduced there as these are set out in full in *Chapter 3*

The incorporation of the Convention into domestic law does *not* change the basis or status of the magistrate's court—but it does require magistrates' who sit in those courts or act in any official capacity to look beyond the national jurisdiction in order to give effective and real protection to the rights set out in the Convention.

Section 3 of the 1998 Act

As indicated in earlier chapters, in order to give effect to Convention rights, the 1998 Act directs courts to interpret national legislation 'compatibly' with the Convention. Section 3 of the Act provides:

(1) So far as it is possible to do so, primary legislation and subordinate legislation must be read and given effect in a way that is compatible with the Convention rights.

(2) This section-
   (a) applies to primary and secondary legislation whenever enacted;
   (b) does not affect the validity, continuing operation or enforcement of any incompatible primary legislation; and
   (c) does not affect the validity, continuing operation or enforcement of any incompatible subordinate legislation if (disregarding any possibility of revocation) primary legislation prevents removal of the incompatibility.

The effect on different types of legislation

It can be seen from section 3 that the 1998 Act has a different effect according to the type of legislation under consideration. In fact, five varieties of legislation can be identified:

- primary compatible legislation;

- primary incompatible legislation;

- secondary compatible legislation;

- secondary incompatible legislation; and

- secondary incompatible but valid legislation.

The Act requires the court to read all legislation in a way compatible with the Convention—'so far as it is possible to do so'. The doctrine of the supremacy of Parliament is thus compromised to that extent—a limited extent—in that courts are given new interpretative powers. What the court must do is first identify *the type* of legislation upon which the criminal proceeding or civil matter is based. It then has to look at the words of the domestic Act or instrument and consider all the possible meanings in the light of both UK law and Convention rights. Perhaps there will be only one possible interpretation. It may be that there are several. Looking at each type of legislation the following points can be made:

- in the case of *primary compatible legislation* the court is free to read the words of the statute so as to give effect to Convention rights.

- in the case of *primary incompatible legislation* the court has no option but to follow the words of the domestic statute notwithstanding that this involves a breach of the Convention. It is not expected that there will be many occasions when the courts cannot interpret compatibly, but when an irreconcilable conflict *does* arise the duty on the court is to follow the words of Parliament and give effect to the statute (i.e. in the full knowledge that this will breach Convention rights).

- in the case of *secondary compatible legislation* the court is free to read the words so as to give effect to Convention rights.

- in the case of *secondary incompatible legislation* the court must interpret the provisions so as to give effect to Convention rights (i.e. even if this requires ignoring the domestic legislation in part or as a whole in order to give effect to such rights). This is an entirely new departure for UK courts.

- in the case of *secondary incompatible but valid* legislation the court must follow the words of the domestic provision even if this involves a clear breach of the Convention. The secondary legislation remains valid because the primary (or 'mother') legislation and the secondary legislation are closely interdependent and the unchallengeable incompatibility of the primary legislation is, in effect, inherited by the secondary legislation—what the Act describes as a situation where 'primary legislation prevents removal of the incompatibility'. The term 'dependent secondary legislation' is encountered in this context.

Understanding the range of interpretative powers available to a court is crucial to understanding how the 1998 Act will work in practice and why it is such a significant piece of legislation.

A hypothetical example

Developing the above themes, consider The Klingon (Registration of Aliens) Act 2003—a wholly imaginary statute. The Act contains a number of provisions dealing with the compulsory registration of aliens in the UK and allows Parliament to set down rules which govern the operation of the Act, which it does in a series of statutory instruments. The Act also allows a public body called the Alien Authority either to register or refuse to register an alien. All unregistered aliens are liable to deportation.

The Klingon (Registration of Aliens) Act 2003 comes into force on 1 January 2004 and section 1 provides that it is an offence to fail to register as an alien with the Alien Authority within 14 days of arrival in the UK. Kluke is an alien. He arrived in the UK in 2002. He does not register with the Alien Authority and when this is discovered he is prosecuted in his local magistrates' court, in February 2004.

Kluke pleads 'not guilty'

Kluke claims that his rights under Article 7 (no punishment without law: see *Chapter 3*) have been breached in that the 2003 Act was not in force at the time he entered the UK. After listening to professional advice the magistrates' court determines that Section 1 of the 2003 Act *does* create retrospective penal legislation. What can they do?

If section 1 can only be interpreted in one way so as to impose on Kluke liability to the sanction of deportation provided for in the Act then it falls within the description 'primary incompatible legislation' and the magistrates must apply the provision in spite of the breach of the Convention. However, if section 1 can be interpreted purposively by reading into it words to the effect that the requirement to register applies only after the Act comes into force then it may fall within the ambit of the term 'primary compatible legislation'. In this event, the magistrates are able to read those words into then 2003 Act thereby providing Kluke with a defence and preserving his rights under the Convention.

Kluke challenges the Alien Authority under the rules

Rule 2 of the Klingon (Registration of Aliens) (Appeal Rules) 2003 allows an alien who is required to register under the Act to appeal to a magistrates' court against the refusal of the Alien Authority to accept the registration. Rule 2(1) states that in determining an appeal the magistrates may take into account any relevant issue as to an alien's character and antecedents. Rule 2(2) does not allow an alien to be represented in the appeal proceedings.

Kluke, having successfully defended the criminal proceedings applies to the Alien Authority for registration. He is refused registration and appeals to the magistrates' court. He brings a lawyer along to the hearing to represent him. The Alien Authority objects, citing the rules already mentioned to the court. What can the magistrates do?

Any prohibition or restriction on Kluke being represented by a lawyer is a clear breach of Article 6 (right to a fair trial). The rule falls within the description secondary incompatible legislation, which because in this instance it is not 'dependent legislation' (which would be valid: above) the justices can set aside. The court may thus ignore rule 2(2) and allow Kluke to be represented in accordance with Article 6.

Kluke's reason for wishing to remain in the UK
Kluke's reason for wanting to register with the Alien Authority is that he has recently married and wishes to remain in the UK. This is the ground he advances in his appeal. The Alien Authority submits that Rule 2(1) prevents the magistrates from hearing about anything other than Kluke's character and antecedents (see above). Kluke's lawyer reminds the court that if his client's appeal is refused he faces the prospect of deportation which will seriously interfere with his rights under Article 8 (right to respect for family life) and that, accordingly, the magistrates must take into account Kluke's full reasons for wanting to register. Furthermore Kluke's lawyer states that for rule 2(1) to be lawful it would be necessary for the Alien Authority to show that the interference with Kluke's family life has a valid basis in law in that it pursues one or more of the aims set out in Article 8(2) (see *Chapter 3*)—and that it is proportionate. He goes on to argue that deportation cannot possibly be proportional to the harm of his failure to register under the Act of 2003.

Perhaps unsurprisingly and having regard also to Article 14 (prohibition of discrimination) the magistrates decide to permit Kluke to give evidence not just of his character and antecedents (as allowed by the rules) but of his recent marriage and desire to make Britain—which he says he believes to be 'an enlightened country'—his new home. By interpreting the Appeal Rules compatibly with rights under the Convention the appeal is allowed by the magistrates.

DECLARATIONS OF INCOMPATIBILITY

Section 4 Human Rights Act 1998 allows a court to make a declaration of incompatibility where it is satisfied that a provision of primary legislation or secondary legislation cannot be interpreted compatibly with a Convention right. Only certain courts can make this declaration and this *does not* include the magistrates' court or the Crown Court.

Such a declaration does not affect the validity, continuing operation or enforcement of the provision in respect of which it is given and it is not binding on the parties in the proceedings in which it is made. In other words a declaration of incompatibility does not allow the court to override primary or 'dependent' secondary legislation and the case must proceed to a conclusion notwithstanding the apparent breach of a Convention right.

Because the first opportunity to obtain a declaration of incompatibility arises at the level of the High Court it seems highly likely that there will be an increasing number of appeals by way of case stated against or applications for judicial review of magistrates' courts' decisions. In time a body of 'Convention friendly' case law will develop. Until then, many areas of practice and procedure are susceptible to challenge.

What happens following a declaration of incompatibility?

Even after a higher court has made a declaration of incompatibility the case in which this occurred must continue to whatever resolution domestic law allows notwithstanding the breach of a Convention right. According to John Wadham, Director of Liberty:[2]

> A declaration of incompatibility will have two effects. First, making a declaration may create public interest and so put pressure on the government to change the law. Secondly, the courts are unlikely to want to make such declarations, which will ensure that they strive to find meanings for statutory provisions that conform to the Convention.

If however a declaration *is* made it triggers a fast track procedure to bring Parliament's attention to the legislative provision in question and which in the opinion of the higher courts offends against the Convention. Section 10 of the 1998 Act empowers a minister of state to lay before Parliament a 'remedial order' without the need to present a Bill to Parliament (followed by its various formal stages through the two Houses). The remedial order is designed to be a speedy and efficient method by which both primary and secondary legislation can be amended. Under the fast track procedure an opportunity is provided for Parliamentary consultation but it is in reality a summary procedure for altering legislation. It was not expected, according to the government during the passage of the Human Rights Act 1998, that Parliament would be required to take advantage of the remedial procedure often.

Declarations of *compatibility*

In an attempt to ensure that future legislation *is* compatible with the Convention (a matter, ultimately, for the courts) all Acts of Parliament will in future carry an endorsement or declaration of compatibility with the Convention. It is expected that—on the hopefully rare occasions

---

[2] *Blackstone's Guide to the Human Rights Act 1998*, John Wadham and Helen Mountfield, 1999.

when Parliament decides to legislate contrary to its obligations under the Convention—a corresponding (but equally non-binding) endorsement to that effect will be included in the offending Act.

INTERPRETING THE 1998 ACT: HOW TO DO IT

As already discussed in *Chapter 2*, English and Welsh courts have been traditionally unused to interpreting legislation *purposively*. However, that approach is not wholly alien. It is possible to draw upon comments made in several cases heard in the House of Lords or by members of the Judicial Committee of the Privy Council (whose jurisdiction as a court of last resort for the Commonwealth has seen many cases involving human rights) in addition to comments made in Parliament as the Human Rights Act 1998 was passed. Thus, e.g. Lord Cooke of Thorndon said that section 3 of the Act

> . . . will require a very different approach to interpretation from that to which the English courts are accustomed. Traditionally, the search has been for the true meaning: now it will be for a possible meaning that would prevent the making of a declaration of incompatibility.

The interpretation of national legislation and the search for a 'possible meaning' so as to give effect to the Convention is at the heart of interpretation once the 1998 Act is in force—and will require the broad and purposive approach (described more fully in *Chapter 2*). The court should not be over-concerned with technicalities, but should look to the *substance* and *reality* of the case. In short, the 1998 Act requires the court to give individuals the fullest measure possible of their fundamental rights.

As an example of the implications of the purposive approach, one of the more controversial suggestions made in the run in to implementation concerns the 'welfare principle' in the Children Act 1989. Section 1 of the 1989 Act provides that in determining any issue affecting the upbringing of a child, his or her welfare is a paramount consideration. Commentators have posed the question whether this principle is compatible with the right to family life in Article 8? Without expressing an opinion either way, it can be noted that it has been suggested a court may—to give effect to that right—wish to read into Section 1 of the 1989 Act the words 'subject to rights arising under the Convention'—thereby allowing it, in appropriate circumstances, to disregard the full force of the welfare principle and weigh the 'equal' rights of parents and children—even if, in most cases, the interests of the child may be allowed to prevail.

REMEDIES IN THE MAGISTRATE'S COURT

Someone whose rights under the Convention have been breached has a right to an effective and real remedy. In many cases it is likely that a remedy can be made available immediately. For example a defendant whose rights have been infringed in the course of a police investigation might be granted an effective remedy by the magistrates excluding evidence unlawfully obtained under Section 78 Police and Criminal Evidence Act 1984 (PACE). Similarly, a non-English speaking defendant appearing in custody having been arrested for the non-payment of a civil debt may—because the Court in Strasbourg is inclined to class proceedings where severe sanctions might be involved as 'criminal'—be entitled to the extra protections in Article 6(3), including an interpreter and an adjournment to another day so that he may properly prepare his defence and consult a lawyer of his own choosing (see further in *Chapters 2* and *5*). In neither case does the recognition of the defendant's rights bring the proceedings to a sudden, dramatic close. The Convention is not 'a villain's charter'.

Sometimes remedies will not be directly available in a magistrates' court even when the court is satisfied that a Convention right has been infringed. The potential remedy may only be available in the higher courts after an appeal. The position where magistrates acknowledge that a provision of legislation involves a breach but are unable to interpret it compatibly has already been mentioned above. The court is bound to follow the incompatible meaning of the legislation. This may cause manifest injustice and magistrates may well be offended by the notion of having to act incompatibly—but that is how the 1998 Act is framed. A particular difficulty is likely to arise at the sentencing stage in criminal proceedings. Should a court accept that there is a breach but because it has no power to interpret in any other way proceed to impose the usual type of sentence—or should the court consider a discharge as opposed to the 'standard' sentence? The latter course is certainly one being promoted as the only effective remedy for an acknowledged breach when a court cannot interpret primary legislation compatibly.

REMEDIES AGAINST MAGISTRATES' COURTS

As indicated in *Chapter 2*, by virtue of section 6 Human Rights Act 1998 it is unlawful for a 'public authority' to act in a way which is incompatible with a Convention right. Both the magistrates' court and the magistrates' court's committee (MCC) fall within the definition of public authority. A victim, or potential victim of such an unlawful act can bring an action against the relevant public authority.

Here, however, it is necessary to distinguish between an act done *administratively* and an act done *judicially*. If a court makes a decision on a matter of law or fact which is subsequently overturned on appeal it is unlikely that the subsequent result on appeal would found an action against the court under section 6. Section 9(3) of the Act specifically excludes liability to pay damages in respect of a judicial act done in good faith. The only exception to this limitation of liability is in respect of damages for wrongful imprisonment. In such cases the state will pay compensation. Both a magistrate and a court clerk/legal adviser appear to be covered by this same limitation in respect of judicial acts. In neither case is there any saving in respect of acts not done in good faith.

The magistrates' courts committee

Decisions taken by the MCC fall squarely within the ambit of administrative functions which may lead to an award of damages if someone's rights have been infringed by failure to act compatibly with a Convention right. Accordingly, administrators of MCCs have a pressing need to ensure that across their range of functions as employers, providers of public services and overall managers of the local magistrates' courts they act compatibly with the Convention.

CONTINUING ROLE OF THE COURT

The Court retains its longstanding oversight function after the 1998 Act comes into force. Someone unable to obtain satisfaction against the state locally for a breach of Convention rights may apply to Strasbourg as before. As emphasised in *Chapter 1*, a main purpose of the Act is to 'bring rights home'—in most cases rendering such journeys unnecessary.

Chapter 4: Human Rights in Practice

Some key points before considering specific areas of the work of the courts in the following chapters. This chapter is about:

- using the 1998 Act to create practical solutions to make the 1998 Act work thereby ensuring that the rights of individual citizens are properly and meaningfully protected by the court process—adopting a *positive* and *purposive* approach

- following a new approach to interpreting and applying existing and future laws in the UK—recognising the assimilation of Convention principles into domestic law by interpreting national laws compatibly whenever possible.

CHAPTER 5

Criminal Law and Procedure

Having looked at the background to the Human Rights Act 1998, the Articles of the Convention and the interpretative powers available to UK courts to give effect to human rights the remaining chapters of this book explore various aspects of the magistrates' court jurisdiction—so as to identify areas where the Convention will be of greatest consequence.

The day-to-day impact is perhaps most significant in relation to criminal law and procedure. Issues under the 1998 Act and the Convention can arise at any stage of the criminal justice process from arrest through to sentence. As explained in *Chapter 2*, the court has a *positive* obligation to ensure that it acts and interprets national law compatibly with the Convention when considering any matter before it, in the present context items such as bail, legal aid, trial issues and sentence. Additionally, an accused person in criminal proceedings is entitled to rely on the Convention where this affords a defence or, e.g. to challenge the admissibility of evidence. The effect will therefore be substantial.

LIBERTY, SECURITY AND A FAIR TRIAL

The two most significant Articles relating to criminal proceedings are Article 5 (right to liberty and security) and Article 6 (right to a fair trial). The remainder of this chapter considers the criminal process from arrest to sentence and looks at areas in which the Convention—and these two Articles in particular—impact upon it. Evidential issues, including those arising on arrest, are covered separately in *Chapter 7*.

Arrest and detention
Article 5 gives everyone the right to liberty and security. This is not an absolute right, however, and can be derogated from in times of emergency. As a general rule it is unlikely that the court will have occasion to consider derogations and accordingly Article 5 is to all intents and purposes an article containing absolute rights.

Under article 5(1) no-one can be deprived of their liberty except in the circumstances prescribed by the Convention. The first of these requirements is that the deprivation of liberty must be in accordance with a procedure prescribed by law.

The Court considered the meaning of 'prescribed by law' in *Sunday Times v. United Kingdom* (1979) 2 EHRR 245 when it held that this means that national law must be sufficiently precise and accessible to the ordinary citizen to enable him or her to regulate their conduct in advance.

Paragraphs (a) to (f) of Article 5(1) (see *Chapter 2*) set out the *only* grounds on which a state can deprive someone of his or her individual liberty. This list is thus exhaustive. Article 5(4) provides that anyone who is deprived of his or her liberty shall be entitled to take proceedings to challenge the lawfulness of the detention. Someone whose liberty has been unlawfully interfered with is also entitled under Article 5(5) to bring proceedings for compensation.

In the United Kingdom the Police and Criminal Evidence Act 1984 (PACE) regulates the powers of the state to arrest and detain people. PACE applies to all authorities responsible for investigating offences and the procedures contained in PACE and its Codes strike a balance between the power of the state to investigate crime and the rights of the citizen to be protected from unfair practices. The Act is familiar to many magistrates and criminal law practitioners—and whilst issues are likely to be raised as to its compatibility with the Convention there is good argument to suggest that the majority of its provisions are compatible with Convention rights and capable of being so read.

Grounds for arrest
Article 5(1)(c) of the Convention sets out the three situations where it is lawful for the state to arrest someone:

(a) where there is a 'reasonable suspicion' that a person has committed an offence;
(b) where it is reasonably considered necessary to prevent a person from committing an offence; and
(c) where it is reasonably considered necessary to prevent a person from fleeing after having committed an offence.

Looking at the scheme for lawful arrests under PACE it is arguable that, generally speaking, national law is Convention compliant. What criminal courts must be particularly careful about is not to allow this general sense of satisfaction to dominate their thinking. Each and every stage of the arrest and detention process must be scrutinised carefully on the individual facts of the case being heard.

(a) Reasonably suspecting the commission of an offence
The requirement of 'reasonable suspicion' mirrors that in national legislation under PACE. Furthermore, Codes of Practice issued

under PACE provide detailed guidance about what can amount to a reasonable suspicion (Code A, para. 1.6-1.7A).

Under the Convention an arrest is lawful if there is a reasonable suspicion that someone has committed 'an offence'. What amounts to an offence has been considered by the Court and interpreted as meaning one created by national criminal law.

Under PACE, a police officer may only arrest someone without a warrant for a serious arrestable offence, carrying five years imprisonment or more, or where general arrest conditions are satisfied under section 25 of the Act. These restrictions of a police officer's powers provide additional protection for the citizen.

(b) Preventing the commission of an offence.
Section 24 of PACE provides that an officer may arrest without warrant anyone who is about to commit an arrestable offence. Again national legislation provides an additional level of protection.

(c) Preventing someone fleeing after committing an offence
This head would appear to be self-explanatory and involves the same type of considerations already outlined.

Reasons for an Arrest
Under Article 5(2) anyone who is arrested has the right to be informed in a language he or she understands of the reasons for his or her arrest and of any charge against him or her. It has been held not be sufficient—as e.g. in *Ireland v. UK* (1978) 2 EHRR 28—simply to tell a suspect that he is being held under emergency legislation. In terms of assessing the compatibility of national law with the Convention it is significant that section 28 of PACE itself makes an arrest unlawful unless the suspect is informed of the arrest and the grounds for it at the time of arrest, or as soon as practicable thereafter.

Right to be brought promptly before a court
The right to be brought promptly before a court is provided for by Article 5(3). In *Brogan v. UK* (1988) 11 EHRR 117, the Court held that there had been a violation of Article 5(3) where the period of detention before reaching court was four days and six hours. That detention had been legally authorised under the Prevention of Terrorism (Temporary Provisions) Act 1984. (Note: the UK has entered a derogation in respect of article 5(3) allowing detention for up to seven days in such cases: *Chapter 3*).

Under PACE, the maximum period for which someone can be detained without charge or appearance before a court is 36 hours.

Thereafter, further detention before charge may only be authorised by a court and usually only after the detainee's appearance before the court.

Section 46 of PACE requires that someone charged with an offence must be brought before a magistrates' court no later than the first sitting after charge or, if no court is sitting, the next day. It is unlikely that these provisions would in themselves violate Article 5(3).

Criminal charges

One of the most important features of Article 6 (right to a fair trial) is the way the Convention protects rights in criminal proceedings to a greater degree than civil rights. The Court has not always agreed with the domestic classification of proceedings as either civil or criminal and it is important to be familiar with the European approach in order to ascertain the rights applicable to someone appearing in court.

The starting point in considering whether proceedings are criminal or civil is to look at the domestic classification of the proceedings and if the state classifies them as civil then to look in more detail at whether the law is of general application, applied by the state and the severity of any penalty arising at the conclusion of the proceedings. It has found the following to be criminal matters:

- proceedings for non-payment of fines or community charge/council tax: *Chapter 8.*

- confiscation proceedings under the Drug Trafficking Offenders Act 1994 or Criminal Justice Act 1988

- proceedings under the Dangerous Dogs Act 1991

- proceedings for the enforcement of maintenance payments: *Chapter 8.*

It seems likely, in view of the above criteria and rulings, that certain proceedings under the Crime and Disorder Act 1998 presently classed as civil matters may have to be recast as criminal. If this is the case the enhanced rights in Article 5 for criminal proceedings will be of equal force including the right to disclosure, legal aid and the presumption of innocence.

Anti-social behaviour orders and sex offender orders are classed as civil orders under national legislation—however, breach of such orders is a criminal offence carrying a penalty of up to five years imprisonment. It thus arguable, owing to the serious criminal sanctions on breach, that the initial proceedings should be treated as criminal rather than civil.

Obviously, where national law classifies proceedings as *criminal* there is a certain pointlessness in defendants arguing that they are civil and attract lesser rights. The Court will treat that classification as conclusive.

Bail

There are a number of similarities between English and Welsh domestic legislation contained in the Bail Act 1976 and Convention rights relating to bail. There are also a number of issues arising under the Convention that could affect the position under the Bail Act 1976.

Right to bail

Under the 1976 Act there is a general right to bail unless there are 'substantial grounds for believing' that one or more of the grounds for refusing bail are made out. Furthermore, the Bail Act requires the court to have regard to other relevant considerations—such as the seriousness of the offence or the defendant's antecedent history—in reaching its decision.

Under the Convention, Article 5(3) provides that everyone arrested or detained on suspicion of committing an offence *shall* be entitled to trial within a reasonable time or to release pending trial 'unless there are relevant and sufficient grounds to justify detention'. The European Court expanded upon the meaning of Article 5(3) in *Wemhoff v. Germany* (1968) 1 EHRR 55 by stating that entitlement to a fair trial within a reasonable time or release are not alternatives and that, unless there are good reasons for refusing bail, the suspect has a right to be released *pending* trial. The tests—under both the Bail Act and the Convention—therefore appear to be broadly similar in that both assume a right to bail unless there are in the former case *substantial* grounds and in the latter *relevant and sufficient* grounds for refusing bail.

Refusal of bail

Under the Convention there are at present only four grounds for refusing bail:

- fear of absconding
- commission of further offences
- interference with the course of justice; and
- the preservation of public order.

The first three of these are mirrored in the Bail Act 1976:

Fear of absconding

It is important to note that the seriousness of the offence and therefore the severity of sentence are not sufficient in themselves to justify a refusal of bail under this ground. Although this is a factor that can be taken into account, the court must look at *all* the circumstances including the background and community ties of the defendant before reaching a decision. In *Mansur v. Turkey* A319 – A (1995) a statutory presumption that people charged with a serious offence are likely to abscond was found to violate Article 5(3).

Commission of further offences

Although the commission of further offences is a ground for refusing bail, the Court in *Clooth v. Belgium* (1991) 14 EHRR 717 required that 'the danger be a plausible one' and that detention must take account of the background, past history and personality of the accused. Furthermore, the court should look at the seriousness of further offences on bail. Previous convictions which are not comparatively serious to the present offence, or commission of further offences that are minor in nature, may not justify a refusal of bail under Article 5(3).

Interference with the course of justice

In line with the provisions of the Bail Act, a refusal of bail can only be justified where a real risk of interference with the course of justice exists. Where that risk diminishes, e.g. after witness statements have been taken or inquiries and investigations are complete, bail should be reviewed to ascertain if this ground still subsists.

Preservation of public order

This ground does not appear in the Bail Act as such and thus cannot on its own provide a ground for refusing bail in UK criminal courts. However, the Court accepted in *Leitellier v. France* (1991) 14 EHRR 83 that in exceptional circumstances a significant risk of public disorder if the accused were to be released could amount to an appropriate ground for refusing bail under the Convention.

Under the Bail Act 1976, there are of course further exceptions to the right to bail, including for the defendant's own protection, the fact that there is insufficient information upon which to take the bail decision and the fact that the defendant is a serving prisoner. These exceptions do not fall directly, or on their own, within the grounds set out in the Convention and as interpreted by the Court. The task for magistrates hearing a bail application is to decide whether a decision to refuse bail on such grounds alone would be compatible with the Convention. As the

1976 Act gives magistrates a discretion, there is strong argument that they should exercise this compatibly with the Convention and grant bail

Repeat bail applications

The Bail Act 1976 contains a prohibition on making more than two bail applications without there being a change of circumstances. Under the Convention someone lawfully detained has the right to have his or her detention reviewed so as to determine whether the reasons for detention still subsist. Arguably national law unjustifiably restricts this right. Whilst the court is required to consider the issue of bail at each and every remand hearing there is no requirement to hear full argument again. This may be tested under the Human Rights Act 1998.

Conditional bail

Under, Article 5(3) 'release may be conditioned by guarantees to appear for trial'. 'Guarantee' means a surety or security. The Court thus recognises sureties and securities as valid conditions of bail. It has gone further stating that if the only objection to bail is a fear of absconding a court must release on bail where guarantees would remove that fear.

Sureties and securities are not of course the only conditions of bail that can be imposed under the Bail Act. The Court has also recognised the surrender of a passport and driving licence as conditions of bail. However, some of the conditions which may from time to time be imposed may themselves involve interference with a right otherwise protected under the Convention. For example, a condition not to enter a particular town might interfere with a person's private or family life under Article 8(1). In such a case the court has to have regard to the conditions in Article 8(2) which permit such interference in certain circumstances. Similarly, the imposition of the bail condition may be well-grounded in law and pursue a legitimate aim—but might affect freedom of association (Article 11), but whatever is it proportional? Could the condition be drafted in a less intrusive way while still, say, protecting a witness or preventing the commission of further offences?

Breaches of bail conditions

The present procedures for establishing whether an offender has breached conditions of bail have several features which do not accord with the Convention. There is no clearly stated standard of proof which the state must satisfy in such proceedings under section 7 Bail Act 1976. The offender is not entitled to an adjournment to prepare his or her defence and it is unlikely that witnesses will be called by the state to allow their evidence to be tested by the offender. Indeed in many cases the court will not even allow the offender to give evidence on his or her own behalf relying solely on representations by his or her legal representative. These apparent breaches of Article 6 (see, generally, *Chapter 3*) caused by a somewhat loose approach to section 7 are quite significant, and it is likely that a challenge will follow soon after the 1998 Act comes into force unless police, prosecutors and courts rethink and refine their practices. It will be no answer to say that there are resource implications, that practices are long established or to construct doubtful excuses for not complying with Convention rights.

Trial within a reasonable time

Article 5(3) provides that anyone detained has the right to a trial within a reasonable time. This is in addition to the more general right under Article 6 to have a charge determined within a reasonable time. Article 5(3) applies to people who are detained and recognises that 'reasonable time' in these cases needs to be more stringent than in those where the accused is on bail. The Court has been reluctant to define 'reasonable time' and has considered each of the cases coming before it on its merits. However, as a general rule delays under two years are not likely to be found to be unreasonable—certainly for more serious or complex offences. Under domestic law, the custody time limits created by the Prosecution of Offences Act 1985 appear to be compatible with the Convention in that, before trial, the maximum period for detention in a magistrate's court is 70 days unless an extension is granted by the court (in circumstances which are likely to be Convention compliant).

Legal aid, representation and interpreters

Article 6(3)(c) gives an accused the right:

(i) to defend himself in person or through legal assistance of his own choosing, or
(ii) to be given free legal assistance when he has insufficient means to pay and the interests of justice require it.

Therefore, an accused person can represent himself or herself—and choose his or her own lawyer, given the means to pay for this. A defendant granted legal aid, however, does not have an unfettered choice. The state may appoint a lawyer, assuming he or she is effective.

Legal aid

Legal aid is available by virtue of Article 6(3)(c) on the condition that the accused has insufficient means and the interests of justice require it. This is similar to the criteria laid down by the Legal Aid Act 1988. The 'interests of justice' test covers a number of factors including complexity, seriousness and the accused's inability to defend himself or herself effectively. The problem lies in those cases which fall outside the scope of the Legal Aid Act 1988. Generally speaking, the enforcement or defence of purely civil rights falls outside the magistrates' court legal aid scheme and courts must look carefully at the legislation to see whether the offending rules are made by secondary legislation which can be ignored in certain circumstances (see, generally, *Chapter 4*).

In *Benham v. UK* (1996) 22 EHRR 293, the Court considered the non-unavailability of legal aid in a case involving committal to prison for non-payment of community charge. It found that this constituted a violation of Article 6 and it stated that the 'severity of the penalty risked by the applicant and the complexity of the applicable law' were factors to be taken into account in determining whether legal aid was required in the interests of justice (i.e. in England and Wales when applying the 'interests of justice' limb of the legal aid test).

In *Hoang v. France* (1922) 16 EHRR 53, the court found that, where there are complex issues to be argued, the interests of justice test requires that the defendant be represented. This may become particularly relevant in the magistrate's courts where defendants apply for legal aid—perhaps for quite minor offences—but are intending to raise convention issues and introduce European case law as part of their defence.

Interpreters

Article 6(3)(e) gives everyone charged with a criminal offence the right 'to have the free assistance of an interpreter if he cannot understand or speak the language used in court'. This right extends not only to the trial but also to pre-trial hearings and to the translation of documents in the proceedings. The court is under an obligation to provide an interpreter to the defendant where this is necessary, without any cost to the defendant regardless of his or her means. The same however cannot be said in what are currently classed as civil proceedings. See further in *Chapter 10*.

Early administrative hearings, early first hearings and trial dates

Under domestic law, a number of new legislative provisions have been introduced aimed at reducing delay and improving effective case management. Whilst these initiatives are to be encouraged and have been proving successful, it is necessary to ensure that at the same time the fair trial guarantees provided by Article 6 are protected. In particular, under Article 6(3)(b) every defendant has the right to have 'adequate time and facilities for the preparation of his defence'. Magistrates and court clerks/legal advisers taking part in 'fast track' courts should always give thought to potential Convention rights issues arising out of the proceedings and, whatever other objectives might be in mind, remain under an overriding duty to give effect to those rights.

Adequate time

Again the Court has been reluctant to place an interpretation on this phrase and each case has been decided on its own facts and merits. However, account can be taken of a number of factors, including the complexity of the case (or lack of it) and whether or not the defendant is represented. In general, however, the Court has been quite restrictive in the amount of time it has allowed for the preparation of a defence.

In *X v. Austria* (1979) 15 DR 160 the Commission found that a period of 17 days was sufficient to prepare for trial. Also in *X v. UK* (1974) 13 YB 314, the court did not find a breach of Article 6(3)(b) where the lawyer met with the client just hours before the trial.

Adequate facilities

The defendant must have the right to communicate freely with his or her lawyer unsupervised. In *Can v. Austria* (1985) 8 EHRR 121, the Court considered that 'adequate facilities' meant 'the accused must have the opportunity to organize his defence in an appropriate way without restriction'.

Magistrates' courts (and their corresponding magistrates' courts committees) will need to ensure therefore that such facilities are provided to the defendant and, as appropriate, his or her lawyer in order to enable the defendant to properly mount and organize his or her defence.

Disclosure

Article 6(3) gives the defendant the right 'to be informed promptly, in a language he understands and in detail, of the nature and cause of the accusation against him'. The principal of *equality of arms* (*Chapter 2*) requires that each party to the proceedings is treated equally and this has particular importance in relation to disclosure.

In *Kaufman v. Belgium* (1986) 50 DR 98 the Commission determined that a party to proceedings should have 'a reasonable opportunity of presenting his case to the court under conditions which do not place him at substantial disadvantage against his opponent'. In *Jespers v. Belgium* (1981) 27 DR 61 the Commission stated that everyone charged with a criminal offence should enjoy 'the opportunity to acquaint himself, for the purpose of preparing his defence, with the result of investigations carried out throughout proceedings and have at his disposal, for the purposes of exonerating himself or of obtaining a reduction in sentence, all elements that have been or could be collected by the competent authorities'. This principle was reiterated in *Edwards v. UK* (1992) 15 EHRR where the court held that it is a requirement of fairness under Article 6(1) that 'prosecution authorities disclose to the defence all material evidence for or against the accused and that failure to do so in the present case gave rise to a defect in the trial process'.

The current national provisions on disclosure are contained in the Criminal Procedure and Investigations Act 1996. In outline, these require that the prosecutor disclose to the defence material that might undermine the prosecution case. The defence might be entitled to further material, known as 'secondary disclosure', which 'might reasonably be expected to assist the accused's defence'. But this secondary disclosure is only available if the defendant has served a defence statement, giving details of his or her defence to the prosecutor. Secondary disclosure by a prosecutor is not therefore automatic and requires service of the defence statement first. It is arguable that this situation in relation to disclosure violates Article 6(1) and (3). Furthermore, the Magistrates' Courts (Advance Information) Rules 1985 require the prosecutor to provide the defence with advance disclosure in either way cases only.

We have already pointed out in *Chapter 2* the potential pitfalls concerning disclosure due to the principle of *equality of arms* (see p.21) The absence of a right to advance information in summary only cases was considered by the High Court in *R v. Stratford Justices, ex parte Imbert* (*The Times*, 25 February 1999). It was held that national law did not infringe the Convention in failing to provide for summary disclosure. However, the case was decided before implementation of the 1998 Act and many commentators doubt whether it was correctly decided in any event. Where a decision of a higher court is the source of the breach of a Convention right, the 1998 Act allows a lower court to ignore that decision so as to give effect to the Convention.

Trial

Article 6 guarantees a right to a fair trial. Some of the specific safeguards provided by the Convention have been covered above, such as adequate time to prepare a defence, the right to be represented and so on. In relation to the trial itself, there are additional safeguards under Article 6 to ensure that it is fair—in particular the right to trial within a reasonable time and the right to call witnesses and to cross-examine witnesses for the other side. Article 6(1) also contains a general right of the accused to participate effectively in the proceedings.

Trial within a reasonable time

In criminal cases the point at which proceedings begin is usually at the time of charge (or when an information is laid with a request for a summons) and they end at the conclusion of the case—with either acquittal or conviction and sentence. A number of factors have been considered by the Court when determining whether a trial has taken place within a reasonable time, including complexity, the conduct of the prosecuting authorities and the conduct of the accused. In *Girolami v. Italy* (1991) the court found that there would be no breach of Article 6 where the proceedings were delayed by the accused, e.g. by his absconding.

In the magistrate's court there is a six months time limit on bringing summary only proceedings although trials can take place well outside this period provided the proceedings are started in time. As far as indictable offences are concerned there is no prescribed period of time after which prosecution is forbidden. However judges have been at pains to remind juries about the special need for caution when relying upon ancient evidence and fading memories. Such safeguards may be acceptable under the Convention.

Right to cross-examine and call witnesses

Article 6(3)(d) provides for the right to test evidence and the right to call evidence on one's own behalf. In accordance with the principle of *equality of arms*, a defendant is entitled to call and examine his own witnesses 'under the same conditions as witnesses against him' and to cross-examine prosecution witnesses. A court will still need to be satisfied that the witness can give relevant evidence and would need to give reasons for any refusal to hear from a witness on the grounds that the evidence was not relevant.

In certain circumstances, the evidence of a witness may be contained in a statement where the witness is in fear (sections 23 and 24 Criminal Justice Act 1988). In such circumstances, the defendant is denied the opportunity to cross-examine (as to which, see *Chapter 7* for further commentary).

Trial in absence

Implicit in a fair trial is the right to 'effectively participate' in the hearing, which as a general principle should mean that the accused is present at the hearing. However, the right to be present is not an absolute one and therefore a trial in the defendant's absence need not necessarily breach the Convention, provided sufficient procedural safeguards are in place to otherwise protect his or her rights.

National law would appear to contain certain Convention compliant safeguards. Under section 10 Magistrates' Court Act 1980 a court shall not proceed to try an information in the absence of the defendant unless it is proved to the satisfaction of the court that the summons was served upon the accused or he or she is otherwise aware of the hearing.

The familiar 'paperwork' procedure for dealing with a vast array of summary offences and under which a defendant may plead guilty by post is likely to be compatible with the Convention because it is a procedure which the defendant may opt for or against by pleading guilty in writing or choosing to attend court to enter a guilty plea or a not guilty plea.

The presumption of innocence and the burden of proof

Article 6(2) provides that everyone charged with a criminal offence shall be presumed innocent until proved guilty according to law. It follows therefore that the burden of proof in criminal proceedings is on the prosecution.

However, under some domestic legislation, the burden is transferred to the defendant when he or she is seeking to establish a defence, e.g. driving a motor vehicle when not insured, or possessing an offensive weapon. In these instances, once the prosecutor has established that the defendant was driving in circumstances that required insurance, or was in possession of an offensive weapon in a public place, the onus is on the defendant to show that he or she either had insurance or had lawful authority or reasonable excuse to have the weapon in a public place. At first glance this construction of legislation appears to violate the Convention. But this reversal of the burden need not necessarily breach Article 6(2). In *Leitgens v. Austria* (1981) 26 DR 171 the Court did not find a violation of Article 6(2) where the general burden of proof remained with the prosecutor but was reversed on one particular element of the offence.

Reasoned judgement

Article 6(1) provides a general obligation on courts to give reasons for their judgements. This is so that, in the spirit of a fair trial, both the defendant and the public at large may know the basis of the decision. This requirement does not apply to juries in the Crown Court but it does apply to magistrates and, in particular, their decisions in summary trials, submissions of no case to answer, admissibility of evidence, bail, sentence and the like. Failure by courts to give reasons on judgement may result in a violation of Article 6(1) and accordingly there will be a need for some changes to the practice in the court. See also *Chapter 10*.

Sentence and costs

The rights guaranteed by Article 6 continue to apply at the sentencing stage of a case but not the presumption of innocence, which is effectively displaced by the court finding the accused guilty or his or her pleading guilty.

Article 3

Certain types of punishment might be considered 'inhuman or degrading' under Article 3 (see *Chapter 3*). However, this tends only to be in extreme cases and relate to the conditions in which the accused serves his or her sentence and not usually to the sentence itself. However, in *Weeks v. UK* 1987 10 EHRR 247, e.g. it was held by the Court that to sentence a 17-year-old to life imprisonment for punitive purposes for an offence of robbery could potentially violate Article 3.

It is perhaps unlikely that Article 3 issues will arise in the magistrates' court on sentence (though they may arise with regard to someones's general treatment at court: see *Chapter 10*).

Article 4

Forced labour and servitude are prohibited under Article 4 of the Convention. This may have an impact on sentences which involve elements of community service and the practice may need to develop of seeking the consent of a defendant to the making of such orders (see p.35). Whilst considering community penalties as a whole there are also issues surrounding electronic tagging and the right to respect for private and family life (Article 8) and certain requirements of probation programmes and the right to freedom of expression (Article 10) which includes the right not to have to express something (a variety of difficulties may arise here as a result of community penalties which require compulsory treatment for either alcohol or drug dependency or active participation in courses or programmes)—and also the need to be precise, e.g. with probation order conditions so as to make it quite certain what is required of the offender. This is not to say that all such items will found a breach the Convention and many of the issues likely to be raised here may be quite spurious or disingenuous—but it important to recognise the breadth of the scope for argument and challenge and it will be necessary to scrutinise each argument and provide reasons for assessing a particular course of action as Convention compliant.

Article 7

This Article prohibits a court from imposing a heavier sentence than that which was available at the time of commission of the offence. Where through legislation the penalty for an offence has increased, the court can only impose a sentence that was in effect and applicable at the time the offence was committed (see also, generally, under Article 7 in *Chapter 3*).

Costs

Under domestic law a defendant is normally entitled to costs following an acquittal. However, the *Practice Direction* (Costs in Criminal Proceedings) 93 Cr. App. R. 89 provides magistrates with a discretion not to order costs where there are positive reasons for this, such as there being 'ample evidence to support a conviction but the defendant is acquitted on a technicality which has no merit'. This might be seen to violate Article 6(2) and the presumption of innocence where a defendant has been acquitted—for whatever reason—and has incurred costs in the course of the proceedings against him or her. In *Sekanini v. Austria* (1993) 17 EHRR 221, the national court took into account a number of suspicions against the defendant when considering his application for costs. The Court found this to be a breach of Article 6(2) and the presumption of innocence.

Chapter 5: Criminal Law and Procedure

Some key points:

- this chapter is about the proper identification of criminal matters according to the Convention and relating the sometimes enhanced Convention rights to criminal proceedings so as to ensure that a fair balance is struck between the state and the individual

- it is also about fairness in criminal proceedings at all stages of the criminal justice process, about proper and equal treatment, from the investigation of offences through to trial and where applicable sentence. But decent and proper treatment is not about creating a 'villain's charter'.

- courts should aim to concentrate on 'bringing rights and justice home' in criminal proceedings, not on purely technical rules

- it would seem that there is a need to 'think through' certain established practices, and in some instances with a degree of urgency.

CHAPTER 6

Human Rights and Family Matters

Family panel magistrates have a wide-ranging jurisdiction to deal with family matters. A main part of this jurisdiction involves dealing with legal proceedings involving the welfare of children. As indicated in *Chapter 1*, the Convention makes no express provision with regard to the rights of children. However, as a general proposition, Convention rights apply equally to *all* individuals irrespective of age. Thus, e.g. parents and children both enjoy the same human rights as individuals and where these conflict it will be for magistrates to resolve the situation. It can also be noted that the Court has been willing to attach considerable weight to the United Nations Convention on the Rights of the Child.

The main rights guaranteed by the Convention which are likely to be raised in the family proceedings court are the right to a fair trial in Article 6 (already outlined in relation to criminal proceedings in the previous chapter) and the protection of private and family life in Article 8 (also touched upon at various points in earlier chapters). Much of the work of the family proceedings court involves applications under the Children Act 1989. Within this chapter aspects of national law which may be problematic are highlighted and examples are given of the application of Convention principles within the field of family law.

Here as in other areas of magistrates' jurisdiction the doctrine of *horizontality* applies: the court —as a public authority—must apply Convention principles when dealing with applications by public bodies *or* private individuals (*Chapter 2*).

The right to family life

There is no doubt that granting any orders under the Children Act 1989 or the Family Law Act 1996 will amount to an infringement of the right to respect for family life contained in Article 8. However, such interference may be justified within the terms of Article 8(2) if it:

- is 'prescribed in law'—When the question will be 'Are the existing criteria for the making of the order clear and specific enough for this?'

- has a legitimate aim—in family proceedings this aim will, in general terms, be the protection of the child under the Children Act 1989 or the applicant under the Family Law Act 1996

- is necessary in a 'democratic society'—A consideration which involves the doctrine of *proportionality* (see, generally, *Chapter 2*).

Ex parte orders

Article 6 deals with the determination of an individual's civil rights and obligations and sets out everyone's entitlement to a fair and public hearing within a reasonable time by an independent and impartial tribunal established by law. The question of infringement of Article 6 may arise in family cases when courts are dealing with *ex parte* applications (sometimes now called 'without notice' applications). Applications for certain orders under the Children Act 1989 and Family Law Act 1996 may be made on an *ex parte* basis. *Ex parte* applications in children cases or affecting occupation of the family home (which can deprive an individual of the right to enter it or require him or her to leave it) should rarely be made and only in the most compelling of circumstances. Decisions by the state to apply for an *ex parte* order in respect of a child are made without involving the parent in the decision-making process. The existing laws and procedures are thus likely to be open to challenge in both these situations.

A fair trial (Article 6) normally involves all parties being given notice of and having the opportunity to attend the hearing. Courts will thus have to be certain that *ex parte* hearings are not heard purely for administrative or other convenience—and that in the case of an emergency protection order concerning a child there will be a real and immediate risk to the child if parents *are* given notice of the hearing and time were to elapses before they could attend. If such applications are granted the reasons for the *ex parte* hearing will need to be recorded with precision along with the reasons why a particular order was or was not made.

Equality of arms

As indicated, Article 6 guarantees parties before the court a fair trial and Artcle 8 the right to family life. In order to achieve this the principle of *equality of arms* has evolved in the Strasbourg Court: *Chapter 2*. Within the specialist field of family law it has been made clear by the courts that non-disclosure of information in Children Act cases should be *the exception* rather than the rule: *Re M* [1998] 2 FLR 1028. It has also been stated that as a matter of procedure any party to whom it is proposed not to reveal information (which can sometimes be highly sensitive) should have the opportunity of making representations to the court. In *Re M* the guardian *ad litem* of the child had sought a direction allowing certain information to be kept from the child's mother. It was stated that the judge ought to have reached a proper balance between the child's welfare and the requirements of the administration of justice. This balancing exercise may need to be revisited in light of *equality of arms*.

In *McMichael v. UK* (1995) 20 EHRR 205 the court considered an application by a father to whom documents—in relation to the freeing of his child for adoption—had not been disclosed. The court had no difficulty in ruling that there had been a breach of Article 6(1) because the national court procedure permitted the decision to be based on documents not revealed to the father—which was additionally a breach of his rights under Article 8 (respect for family life).

One area of family law could prove problematic following the decision in *Re L* (1996) 1 FLR 731 where it was confirmed that on granting leave for the disclosure of papers to an expert that expert's report must be filed and disclosed even where disclosure would be contrary to the client's interest. By a *Practice Direction* in 1995 the President of the Family Division of the High Court stated that a duty is owed to the court both by the parties and their legal representatives to give full and frank disclosure in all matters in respect of children. The question the court will have to consider is does this create an unfair trial (i.e. if a party is required to disclose an adverse report) and thus infringe Article 6? To ensure the applicant receives a fair trial it can be argued that he or she should be able to take advice from third parties, in addition to his or her lawyer, in confidence and that if a report is unfavourable he or she should not be compelled to disclose it.

Right to information
The right to information was considered to be an aspect of family life protected by Article 8 in *Gaskin v. UK* (1989) in relation to access to records kept by a local authority in respect of a child in their care. The Court said that 'persons in the position of the applicant have a vital interest, protected by the Convention, in receiving the information necessary to know and understand their childhood and early development'. At present under our domestic law access to records is limited.

Access to a court
Article 6 (right to a fair trial) does not specifically provide for a right of access to a court. However it is recognised that inherent in the right to a fair trial is the fundamental one of access to justice. Within certain areas of national child law access to the courts is restricted. For example, within the field of private law (applications by individuals as opposed to the state: see later in this chapter) some family members such as grandparents do not have direct access to the courts. They must first apply for leave to make an application under section 8 Children Act

1989. However, the Court has upheld restrictions on the right of access to courts provided these have a legitimate aim and comply with the concept of proportionality. In *Golder v. UK* (1975) 1 EHRR 524 restrictions placed on a prisoner's access to the court were considered justified.

In another case, the Court considered an application by a mental patient which required leave of the court before he could start proceedings. It held that

> certainly the right of access to the courts is not absolute and may be subject to limitations . . . the right of access by its very nature calls for regulation by the state which may vary in time and place according to the needs and resources of the community and of individuals . . . the contracting states enjoy a margin of appreciation [see *Chapter 2*] . . . a limitation will not be compatible with Article 6(1) if it does not pursue a legitimate aim and if there is no reasonable relationship of proportionality between the means employed and the aim sought to be achieved.

The criteria set out in section 10(9) Children Act 1989 (which deals with applications for leave to apply for a section 8 order) would appear to contain such balancing criteria.

A further area for consideration under domestic legislation is the limited access to a court afforded to children. Children have the right to apply for leave to issue proceedings under section 8 Children Act 1989 but—even if the child has sufficient understanding—leave may not be given. These are matters which will in time have to be addressed by the higher courts in the UK (applications by children cannot be dealt with in the magistrates' family proceedings court or the county court).

An issue that *is* likely to be raised in the family proceedings court is whether or not the child can attend court where there are proceedings involving him or her. Whilst in civil law there is no general right to be present at court, where issues which affect fundamental rights, such as the right to family life are raised (e.g. decisions about contact with children and their being taken into care by a local authority), then the right to attend court may be protected. Current UK national law, which discourages the attendance of the child may need to be re-examined in the light of this.

Similarly, another question that the court will be asked to consider is whether an order of the court under section 91(14) Children Act 1989 (that no application for an order under the Children Act may be made with respect to the child concerned without the leave of the court) would conflict with the right of access to a court contained in Article 6(1). In *F v. Kent County Council* [1993] 1 FCR 217 the court held that the exercise of judicial discretion under section 91(14) should be used sparingly and in situations where applications are being made too often and where the other party and the child are seen to be suffering from them, or are likely to suffer if such applications continue. The right of access to the court is not absolute and *Golder v. UK* (above) recognised that restrictions may be imposed. It is unlikely that orders under section 91(14) will infringe Convention rights under Article 6(1), as the applicant is not being denied access to the courts, rather access is being restricted upon valid grounds.

Public hearing

A further matter which stems from Article 6 is the entitlement of a party to proceedings to have his or her rights determined at a hearing held in public. The right may be qualified and it can easily be argued that the protection of a child's interest is a legitimate aim permitting the restriction of this right by making the hearing of such matters a private matter. However, while the press and public may be excluded from hearings in the circumstances prescribed under Article 6(1) — in the interests of morals, public order or national security in a democratic society, where the interests of juveniles or the protection of the private life of parties so require, or to the extent strictly necessary in the opinion of the court in special circumstances where publicity would prejudice the interests of justice — these provisions are not expressly applied to the judgement of the court.

So far, there is no clear guidance on this from Strasbourg. The essential objective of Article 6 is the right to a fair *hearing*. The purpose underlying publicity in this context is to ensure scrutiny of the judiciary by the public with a view to safeguarding that right. There is an obvious tension between this part of Article 6 and Article 8 (right to respect for private and family life). If judgements were to be pronounced publicly this could inevitably involve the recital of sensitive material in order that the appropriate and necessary findings of fact could be understood. Therefore the rationale of conducting a hearing in private (e.g. interests of juveniles and protection of the private life of parties) could be undermined—and, as already indicated, it could be argued that there would be an infringement of Article 8.

It is worth noting that rule 16(7) Family Proceedings Courts (Children Act 1989) Rules 1991 implies that the court has a duty to actively consider whether it is expedient in the interests of the child to hear proceedings in private, when only the officers of the court, the parties, their legal representatives and other people specified by the court may attend.

Delay

An aspect of the right to a fair trial is the right to have civil and criminal proceedings determined within a reasonable time. Enshrined within the body of the Children Act 1989 is the general principle that any delay in determining any question with respect to the upbringing of a child is likely to prejudice the welfare of that child. However, a planned and purposeful delay to enable a proper assessment to be undertaken may well be beneficial. Family proceedings courts are only too familiar with cases that can take from three months to two years to determine. Will such delays amount to a breach of Article 6? Whilst much depends on the individual circumstances of each case, it can be said with some degree of certainty that delays based on heavy workload or an absence or shortage of resources are unlikely to be justifiable: see *Zimmerman v. Switzerland* 1983 6 EHRR 17. In the face of a delay, a court is likely to have to balance the reasons for this against the infringement of any other rights (e.g. the risk of harm to the child) before deciding whether the delay is unreasonable, and certainly before deciding what remedy can be given to someone whose rights to an expeditious determination are being infringed. The need to avoid delay is likely to require courts to undertake more pro-active case management.

Care proceedings

Although many aspects of modern English family law are likely to be compliant with the Convention, given the nature of the work and the specific references to respect for family life in Article 8 it is likely that incorporation of the Convention will have a considerable impact.

Removal of a child from his or her family is perhaps the most serious interference with family life. One of the objectives of Article 8 is to protect the individual against arbitrary action by public authorities: *Kroon v. Netherlands* 1995 19 EHRR 263. Family life is seen as a self-regulating area into which the state should not intrude except where fully justified. Such justification must be on one of the grounds contained in Article 8(2):

- the interests of national security
- public safety or the economic well being of the country
- for the prevention of disorder or crime
- for the protection of health or morals
- for the protection of the rights and freedoms of others; and also
- restrictions and interferences must be clearly defined, logically justified and the minimum necessary to achieve a legitimate objective. As indicated earlier, courts will, when determining whether the interference can be justified, have to apply the following structure:

—Is the interference in accordance with the law?
—Does it serve a legitimate aim?
—Is it necessary in a democratic society?

Clearly under UK national law the interference is prescribed by law and it will have a legitimate aim, the protection of a child's health, rights and freedom. The Strasbourg case law emphasises that the interference must be *necessary*, not just *desirable* and that the interference must correspond to a pressing social need and be proportionate to the legitimate aim pursued *Silver v. UK* [1983] 5 EHRR 344.

Balancing rights

Prior to looking at the orders of the court and the duty placed upon it by the Human Rights Act 1998 to interpret legislation compatibly with the Convention it is useful to consider what is known as the 'child protection conference' where the local authority consults a range of agencies before deciding what action to take, if any, concerning a child who appears to be at risk in the family home. Failure to consult parents or other relevant people may be a violation of Article 8, which needs to be justified, whether or not the public authority has a statutory obligation to consult under national law. Where decisions are taken in the absence of parents, it will be open to them to claim there has been an unjustifiable violation of their rights.

When a court is dealing with applications to take children into care, there appears to be little doubt that the protection of a vulnerable child is of paramount importance and is justification for that interference. In *Johansen v. Norway* (1996) 23 EHRR 333 the court held that the taking and keeping of a child in care did not breach Article 8 (right to family life). Within the decision-making process a fair balance will have to be struck between the competing interests. In this balancing exercise, particular importance will be attached to the best interests of the child which, depending on their nature and seriousness may override those of the parent. Under current national law the child's welfare is a court's paramount consideration. Will this principle be open to challenge under Article 8 on the basis that the parents' family rights should be on a par with those of the child? A review of the decisions of the Commission shows that it has consistently taken the view that 'where . . . there is a serious conflict between the interest of the child and one of its parents, which can only be resolved to the disadvantage of one of them, the interests of the child must [under Article 8(2)] prevail: *Hendricks v The Netherlands* (1983) 5 EHRR 223. This follows the United Nations Convention on the Rights of the Child. Similarly in *Johansen v. Norway* (above) the Court recognised that the best interests of the child were of 'crucial importance'.

Contact with children in care

Under the Children Act 1989 there is a duty to allow reasonable contact between parents and children. The court has power under section 34(4) to authorise a local authority to refuse to allow contact between a child and members of its family. In practice the concept of parental rights has been given little weight in UK courts and in some cases a court's hands would seem to have been tied where a local authority's 'care plan' (see below) is for adoption of the child. In *Johansen v. Norway* (above) the applicant's child was taken into care on the basis that she was incapable of taking care of her daughter. The mother was later refused access to her child as she had been placed in a foster home with a view to adoption. The mother complained that there had been a breach of both Article 6 (right to a fair trial) and Article 8 (right to respect for private and family life). The Court held that taking and keeping a child in care did not infringe Article 8, but that deprivation of contact by the mother with her child did. Among other things, denying contact ruled out the possibility of rehabilitation. Taking children into care should normally be regarded as a temporary measure to be discontinued as soon as circumstances permit. The termination of parental contact may, however, be justified on the ground that it really is contrary to the interests of the child—as where there is a risk of physical, psychological or emotional abuse continuing and which might lead to long-term damage to the child.

Care plans

The most glaring difficulty in this field of law is the inability of the courts to go behind a local authority care plan. Monitoring by the courts of a child in care has been specifically excluded by national case law. At present the court cannot interfere with such plans once a care order has been made, even if these plans change rapidly after a care order is made. It is also a matter of concern that the court is often faced with a stark choice in some instances of accepting a care plan—with all its possible limitations—or refusing to make a care order. Since so many decisions concerning parents' and children's rights depend on such a care plan it is arguable that it cannot be in conformity with the Convention for a court to be unable to look *behind* the plan when determining Article 8 rights.

Children and private law proceedings

Private law cases are those which involve disputes between parents or family members rather than intervention by a local authority. The overriding issue in this area of the law is the right of the child and parent to develop a relationship with each other. Contact, in English law, has developed as the *right of the child* to have contact with its parents, not the *right of the parents* to see the child. Under national law the focus of the court is on the welfare and best interests of the child—and contact is seen as furthering that welfare and those interests. The courts may and often do act against the wishes of the child.

Under Article 8 the emphasis is on the *right to respect for family life*. In *Peter Whitear v. UK* (1997) EHRLR 291 the Commission recognised in principle that a parent always has a right of contact with his or her child under that Article—which would appear to challenge the conventional approach in national courts that parents do not have rights of contact.

Strasbourg case law has emphasised that in principle a parent normally has a right of access to his or her child. Contact and residence decisions must be justified, necessary and proportionate. Once again the court will have to balance the rights of the child with those of the parents. The rights of the parents will need to be addressed alongside the national law principle that the welfare of the child is paramount—in the main body of the court's recorded reasons for making its decision.

Chapter 6: Human Rights and Family Matters

Some key points:

- this chapter is about recognising that Article 6 (right to a fair trial) and Article 8 (right to family life) are always engaged in family proceedings

- this applies in both private and public law proceedings and may require courts to rethink some of their most basic premises

- a proper balance must be struck between the parties, and between the parties and the rights of other people—and it is particularly important to do this in relation to parents and children whose rights under the Convention are on a par

- often, the court may need to consider the legitimate aim of the proceedings, the principle of *proportionality* and what exactly is necessary in a democratic society.

CHAPTER 7

The Convention and Evidence

The Lord Chancellor has given advice to his local Advisory Committees on the appointment of magistrates that in determining the number of new appointments needed in 2000 they should—as a result of the Human Rights Act 1998—expect a four per cent increase in the workload of the Magistrates' Courts Service. This will result mainly from the time taken to deal with trials of cases following pleas of 'not guilty'. In this context, the number of evidential points taken as a result of the Convention is likely to increase sharply. In this chapter we look at just some of evidential issues which are likely to be argued—as a guide to the kind of submissions, Convention-based considerations and thinking which will affect this aspect of court work once the 1998 Act is in force.

Hearsay / documentary evidence

Criminal proceedings
In criminal trials, the key Articles affecting the admissibility of and weight to be given to this kind of evidence are Article 6(2) (the presumption of innocence) and Article 6(3)(d) (which states that any one charged with a criminal offence shall be entitled to examine or have examined witnesses against him or her and to obtain the attendance and examination of witnesses on his or her behalf under the same conditions as the witnesses against).

The Convention itself is silent on the direct question of hearsay, but it can be argued that, on a literal interpretation, hearsay evidence should not be admitted—because it is by definition not the evidence of a witness but of someone else. The Strasbourg institutions have not taken this line and have allowed national courts to rely on hearsay evidence—but only if there are counterbalancing factors which preserve the rights of the defence: *Barbera, Messegue and Jabardo v. Spain* (1989) 11 EHRR 360. The Court asks whether the whole trial has been fair. As a general rule, however, any conviction based solely or mainly on hearsay evidence is likely to violate article 6(3)(d).

The case of *Van Mechelen and Others v. Netherlands* (1997) 25 EHRR 647 also sets out a new principle, namely that:

> . . . any measures restricting the rights of the defence should be strictly necessary. If a less restrictive measure can suffice than that measure should be applied.

For hearsay evidence not to offend Article 6(3)(d) what sort of counterbalancing procedures to protect the rights of the defendant are needed? Two contrasting cases may give some understanding of the approach by Strasbourg. Both involve a situation where witnesses were allowed to be anonymous because of the fear of reprisals against them.

In *Kostovski v. The Netherlands* (1989) 12 EHRR 434 the evidence of two anonymous witnesses was taken by examining magistrates and then presented as hearsay evidence at the applicant's trial. The defence had not been present before the examining magistrate but had been able to submit written questions. The police and examining magistrate were available for cross-examination at the trial. The threats to the witnesses were real but the European Court found the procedures 'irreconcilable with the guarantees contained in Article 6'.

In *Doorson v. Netherlands* (1996) 22 EHRR far more stringent counterbalancing factors found favour with the Court. Anonymous witnesses were questioned by an investigating magistrate in the presence of the applicant's counsel who could put through the magistrate any question except those that could lead to the identity of the witness.

The relevant law in England and Wales dealing with the admissibility of documentary hearsay evidence is contained in sections 23 to 24 Criminal Justice Act 1988. Section 23 allows documentary evidence to be admitted if certain criteria exist explaining the absence of the witness (examples being that the witness fears reprisals, is abroad, or has died). Section 24 deals with the admissibility of business documents. Section 25, however, gives the court a discretion not to admit such evidence and sets out criteria for the court to consider when exercising that discretion. These criteria in summary trials are to ensure that the defendant is not unfairly treated when the court is considering whether to exercise its discretion.

It is arguable that these provisions will not fall foul of Article 6. However courts would be well advised to be aware of the judgement in *Van Mechelen* above and to exercise great caution in admitting such evidence if it is likely to be the only or major part of the evidence against the accused.

The Convention should not have any affect on agreed statements (such as 'section 9 statements') and defence admissions of fact since here the defendant has an unfettered right to decide whether or not to agree to these being admitted in evidence, with legal advice if need be (and they are not, technically speaking, hearsay).

Civil cases
In civil cases (within the meaning attributed to this phrase by the Strasbourg institutions) the specific right given by Article 6(3)(d)

(examination and cross-examination of witnesses) is not applicable. However, Strasbourg has still required such proceedings to be fair and will examine whether the introduction of hearsay evidence renders a trail unfair. The admissibility of hearsay evidence in civil matters with the exception of Children Act 1989 proceedings is now governed by the Civil Evidence Act 1995. This states that all hearsay evidence is admissible providing the requirements as to notice to be found in that Act are complied with. Section 4 of the 1995 Act sets out criteria to be used by the courts as to the weight to be given to such evidence. These criteria effectively lay down a balancing exercise for the court—weighing the reason for the introduction of such evidence against unfairness to the opposite party. On the face of it, the 1995 Act would seem to acknowledge the 'balancing exercise' required by Strasbourg when hearsay evidence is being considered. The only possible objection is that it allows —hearsay evidence to be admitted—the criteria only affect the *weight* to be attached to that evidence. However, section 3 of that Act does allow the court on application to insist on the witness being present and providing this discretion is exercised to ensure civil trials are fairly conducted Article 6 would seem to be complied with.

Inferences from silence

The provisions of sections 34 to 37 Criminal Justice and Public Order Act 1994 may be open to challenge under Article 6. These sections allow courts to draw inferences where a defendant in a criminal trial does not give evidence at his or her trial or fails to answer questions put to him or her by the police in the pre trial process etc. The Court in *Murray v. United Kingdom* (1996) 22 EHRR 29 considered a similar provision in Northern Ireland. The applicant had argued that the right to draw inferences breached the presumption of innocence provided for by Article 6(2), but the Court rejected this argument. However it did hold that the Article *was* breached when the power to draw inferences was combined with the absence of a solicitor in the police station at the time when the defendant was being questioned. In rejecting the direct challenge (i.e. that it was contrary to Article 6(1) to ever allow inferences to be drawn from silence) the Court emphasised that the independent evidence of guilt was strong. The Northern Ireland legislation had a number of safeguards, and the trial was before a judge sitting without a jury who had to a give reasoned judgement which was open to challenge.

It is by no means clear whether a challenge based on magistrates drawing inferences under ss. 34 to 37 would fail. The Home Office has issued a circular to the police as a result of the Northern Ireland case. When a suspect is interviewed in the absence of a legal adviser, a further interview should take place when a legal adviser arrives, giving the suspect a further right to comment and so on.

This area of law is in truth far from clear and at the time of writing there are a number of cases pending before the Court against the UK which seek to challenge the practical operation of sections 34 to 37 (e.g. *Hamil v UK* Application 21656/93 (1997) EHRR 169 and *Kevin Murray v. UK* Application 22384/93 (1997) EHRR 169). Their determination in due course should clarify matters.

The right to silence

Irrespective of whether someone can have inferences drawn from being silent it seems clear that it will be a breach of Article 6 to compel someone to answer questions if the results of those questions are then used against him or her in a subsequent trial. In *Saunders v. UK* (1997) 23 EHRR 313 the applicant was a director at Guinness and had been questioned under threat of punishment if he refused answers to Department of Trade and Industry inspectors under the Companies Act 1985. The results of this questioning were used by the prosecutor at a subsequent trial for false accounting and conspiracy. The Court found that there was a breach of Article 6. It stressed that the right not to incriminate oneself lay at the heart of the concept of a fair trial within the meaning of Article 6.

This general principle may not feature regularly in magistrates' courts. It is perhaps more likely to do so in respect of an either way or indictable offence, and submissions concerning the principle could be put in proceedings to commit a case to the Crown Court for trial.

Unlawfully obtained evidence

The relevant domestic law concerning unlawfully obtained evidence is contained principally in sections 76 and 78 of the Police and Criminal Evidence Act 1984 (PACE). Section 78 allows a court to declare evidence inadmissible if to admit it would have an adverse effect on the fairness of the trial. The House of Lords in the leading case of *R v. Sang* (1980) AC 402 (1979); 2 All ER 46 indicated that in exercising it's discretion the court should consider whether the probative effect of the evidence outweighs its prejudicial effect. Therefore in cases where the police/prosecution have clearly obtained evidence unfairly it could still be admitted under this ruling. Under section 76 of PACE 'confessions' can only be admitted where the prosecutor shows that the evidence has not been obtained by oppression or in circumstances where it, the confession, would be unreliable.

When the Human Rights Act 1998 is in force, magistrates will have to decide whether to admit evidence where it has been obtained in breach of the Convention. The Strasbourg institutions have not ruled that there is an absolute prohibition against such evidence being admitted. They again look at the overall fairness of the trial and consider such matters as how the evidence was obtained, how serious is the breach of the Convention, and its impact on the overall fairness of the trial.

At the time of writing, the Court is considering *Khan v UK* which is likely to clarify whether evidence obtained in breach of the Convention must be excluded. In the meantime, some further guidance drawn from decisions of the Court can be proffered:

- if the evidence unlawfully obtained is the only or major part of the evidence against the accused, it is less likely to be admitted than if it is only a minor part of the evidence against him or her.

- evidence obtained in breach of absolute rights (such as Article 3: prohibition of torture etc.) and evidence which, of itself, breaches Article 6 (such as where an undercover agent incites criminal offences) is again unlikely to be regarded as admissible.

- as regards confession evidence, *G v. UK* Appl. 9370/81, 35 DR 75 indicates—as the Commission emphasised—that there is a need for early access to a lawyer if confessions are to be admitted.

The *voir–dire*

In English law the judge hears submissions made by the defence that evidence should be declared inadmissible in the absence of the jury. If the evidence is declared inadmissible the jury—the judges of fact—do not hear that evidence at all. In *G v. UK* above the Commission found this procedure for dealing with submissions about confession evidence satisfactory especially in view of the fact that the burden of proving that the statement was voluntary fell to the prosecutor.

In summary trials in the magistrates' court, magistrates are judges of both fact and law. If they decide that evidence is inadmissible they continue to hear the case even though they have heard the offending information. Whilst they are appointed because of their ability to adopt a judicial attitude (i.e. notionally they can put the information from their minds so that it does not affect their eventual evidence-based decision) and they receive training in this regard, challenges are likely from October 2000 on the basis that they cannot really then be perceived to be a fair and impartial tribunal as required by Article 6. In cases which are triable either in the Crown Court or the magistrates' court this problem can be overcome by committing the case to the Crown Court for trial. In purely summary cases it is difficult to see how it can be surmounted without changes to primary legislation.

Disclosure

As has already been outlined in earlier *Chapters*, under existing English law the prosecutor in purely summary cases is not obliged to disclose the case against the accused (in contrast to the position in relation to either way offences). Under the *equality of arms* doctrine there should be a fair balance between parties involved in legal proceedings (*Chapter 2*).

In *Edwards v. UK* (1992) 15 EHRR 417 disclosure by the prosecutor was seen by the European Court as a crucial precondition of a fair trial. However in *R v. Stratford Justices, ex parte Imbert* (*The Times*, 25 February 1999) the defendant charged with a summary offence sought a stay of the proceedings against him on the basis that a fair trial within the meaning of Article 6 required advance, pre–trial disclosure by the prosecutor of witness statements.

The High Court upheld the decision of the magistrates' court not to allow such a stay. Lord Justice Buxton said that the outcome would have been no different had the case been decided under the Human Rights Act 1998. Virtually all commentators on this case, however, believe it to have been wrongly decided and it is almost certain that the issue will have to be reconsidered by the higher courts in the UK when the 1998 Act is actually in force. If ultimately found to be a breach of Article 6, it is arguable that magistrates should order the prosecutor to disclose his or her case and if he or she declines to do so then to stay the proceedings as an abuse of the court process.

In practice this issue will only arise in areas of the country where the prosecutor is unwilling to make voluntary disclosure: in most areas prosecutors *will* disclose relevant information voluntarily in summary cases.

Chapter 7: The Convention and Evidence

Some key points:

- this chapter is about reviewing and testing the rules of evidence against the Convention model of a fair trial

- it is also about ensuring that the conduct of any trial is carried out fairly by respecting and balancing the rights of the individual to freedom of action against the rights of the state to maintain public order and the rule of law

- courts must establish a clear framework in which the right to a fair trial for everyone is governed by rules of evidence which are clear, fair and equal in their content, nature, application and extent.

CHAPTER 8

The Convention and Enforcement

Magistrates' courts often have to enforce their own orders or those of other courts. The majority of such orders involve the payment of money due in criminal or civil proceedings, but this is not the only type of enforcement. Family proceeding courts, in particular, must enforce different types of orders, primarily those regulating contact between children and parents, non-molestation orders and occupation of the family home. Sometimes enforcement can occur in either a family proceedings court or the ordinary magistrates' court.

It is clear that the Convention will play a significant role in the enforcement process. Indeed, there have already been rulings—briefly mentioned in *Chapter 3*—concerning the community charge and maintenance payments—which are having a major impact on enforcement proceedings. These will now be considered in greater detail.

COUNCIL TAX AND COMMUNITY CHARGE

The introduction of the community charge in 1989 proved unpopular with many people. Perhaps inevitably, issues surrounding the enforcement of the charge came to the attention of the Court, initially in *Benham v UK* (1993) 22 EHRR 293. Mr Benham had appeared before magistrates for non-payment of the community charge and the court was considering committing him to prison. He applied for legal aid but this was refused by the clerk to the justices on the basis that these were civil proceedings and legal aid was unavailable. He was duly committed to prison following which he applied to the Court against both the decision to commit him and refusal of legal aid.

The Court found that the decision to commit was proper. The power to do so was clearly laid down in national law and Article 5(1)(b) of the Convention allows for lawful detention for non-compliance with a lawful order of a court. However, the decision to refuse legal aid was wrong and Mr Benham's application on that ground was allowed. The Court did not accept as correct the domestic law classification of the proceedings as civil. The Court said:

> In view of the severity of the penalty risked by the applicant and the complexity of the applicable law the Court considers that the interests of justice demand that, in order to receive a fair hearing, the applicant ought to

have benefited from free legal representation during the proceedings before the magistrates.

In conclusion there had been a violation of Article 6(1) and (3)(c) of the Convention.

The impact of the *Benham* case has been far reaching. Courts have established working arrangements with local duty solicitor schemes to cover all types of default case where the court is considering committal to prison for non-payment. The case also shows what factors the Court of will consider when deciding whether proceedings are *civil* or *criminal*. Readers are reminded that if proceedings are considered 'criminal' then the 'extra' rights contained in Article 6(2) and (3) automatically apply. A risk of custody would seem to suggest that in most case the Court would classify the proceedings as criminal.

This approach of the Court coincides with recent decisions of the High Court emphasising that the main purpose of enforcement legislation is to collect the debt. Since prison can wipe out the debt, it should, in any event, only be used as a last resort.

FINE ETC. ENFORCEMENT

The fine is the most common sentence imposed by magistrates' courts and its enforcement is therefore of considerable importance. The budget allocated to a magistrates' courts committee is also affected by performance in this area. The Convention has (and in future may) affect many aspects of this work.

Fine enforcement and proportionality

Many fines which are enforced are for relatively minor offences. Perhaps the most obvious regular example is the enforcement of fines imposed for not having a TV licence. A survey by the Justices' Clerks' Society in 1996 showed that two thirds of defendants in such cases were women. Many were single parents in receipt of state benefits and over 90 per cent of all women appearing in a defaulters court do so as a result of this one offence. In such cases the use of imprisonment, albeit as a last resort, might well fall foul of the rule about proportionality (*Chapter 2*). Will the Court ever consider the imprisonment of someone in such circumstance to be proportional? The *Benham* case, by analogy, shows that these proceedings will be regarded as criminal if custody is being considered and duty solicitor schemes throughout the country should provide cover for such cases. It is arguable, however, that the overall fairness of the procedure may be open to challenge.

Section 82(3)(6) Magistrates Court Act 1980 makes it clear that save in certain circumstances a person cannot be imprisoned for non-payment unless a means inquiry has been held in the defendant's presence on at least one occasion. The means inquiry is therefore a crucial stage in the enforcement process. At present, the justices' clerk not only brings the proceedings and either personally or through a legal adviser conducts the means inquiry in court by asking defendants why they have not paid and giving details of the defendant's finances (often also providing a payment history or lack thereof from court records) but also advises the court.

In *R v. Corby Justices ex parte Mort* (1998) 162 JP 310 the Divisional Court was asked to rule on the fairness of this procedure. The applicant challenged the arrangement whereby the legal adviser asked her questions about the non-payment of fines and thereafter proffered advice to the adjudicating magistrates. The Divisional Court examined the 1980 Act and concluded that the requirement for a means inquiry meant that either the magistrtates or the clerk had to conduct it—and the clerk had to do so in order to leave the magistrates free to make the decision on enforcement. It said that in conducting the inquiry the clerk needed to avoid an adversarial and partisan role and should not set out to establish wilful refusal or culpable neglect to pay (the criteria for custody) in the manner of his or her questioning. The Divisional Court concluded that the dual role of the adviser did not impugn the fairness of the proceedings and dismissed the application; it also doubted whether the Convention would bring a different result.

The applicant has now taken her case to Strasbourg and the Lord Chancellor's Department is having to consider what procedures will need to be put in place if the Court rules against the UK. One possibility is to have a member of the accounts staff responsible ultimately to the justices' chief executive (i.e. as head of the staff of the magistrates' courts committee as opposed to being responsible as a clerk to justices is for legal advice) to present the case in court and to question the defendant. Under the Convention, he or she would also have to be prepared to be questioned by the defendant or his or her legal representative. However, even these changes may still be open to challenge since both the presenter and legal adviser would still have been appointed by and 'owe allegiance' to the same MCC. The ultimate consequence of an adverse ruling by the Court could be that enforcement of fines etc. has to be administered completely independently—possibly by an outside agency.

Other potential bases for challenges under the Convention
One common method of fine enforcement is issuing a distress warrant to seize and sell off the defendant's goods. In *R v. Hereford and Worcester*

Justices, ex parte Macrae (1998), *The Times,* December 31, the Divisional Court stressed the importance of collecting the debt rather than losing it by imprisonment and said that a court's use of distress warrants was crucial. It is possible there may be challenges to the issue of distress warrants claiming breaches of Article 8 (right to respect for family life) and the First Protocol, Article 1 (peaceful enjoyment of possessions). Claims of breaches of the latter Article may be hard to establish, as the Article is a qualified right. The state is allowed to enact laws relating to the payment of taxes, or other penalties. The concept of *proportionality* could however be argued. A distress warrant issued for a small sum for a minor matter could be open to challenge along the lines already explained earlier in this chapter.

Challenges under Article 8 are more likely. In *McLeod v UK* (1999) EHRLR police officers had entered Mrs Michael's house to allow her husband to remove property following a court order dividing the matrimonial assets. However, the police had not verified her ex-husband's entitlement to enter the house and as Mrs Michael was not there at the time the police officers' fears of a breach of the peace were not made out. Their entry was not proportionate to the legitimate aim pursued. Bailiffs however will have a distress warrant which gives them the legal authority to enter premises for a specific purpose. As a matter of public policy their entry is likely to be in the interest of society and consistent with Article 8(2); it is in society's interest that court orders are met with compliance and the Divisional Court in the *Macrae* case sanctioned the use of distress.

Finally, there is the question whether there is a fair trial if a distress warrant is issued without a hearing as part of what might be described as 'automatic' enforcement procedures, or even whether later enforcement by way of a means inquiry could be tainted by such a defect at an earlier stage.

MAINTENANCE PAYMENTS

In *Eusebio Santa Cruz Ruiz v. UK* (Application No. 261 09/95) maintenance enforcement proceedings were classified as 'criminal' when custody was being considered. The Access to Justice Act 1999 (when implemented) will transfer to the justices' chief executive the court collecting functions which currently rest with the justices' clerk (i.e. responsibility for maintenance and similar civil payments). However, again, since the former is closely connected with the latter similar question marks over the fairness and impartiality of enforcement proceedings will remain if there is an adverse ruling in the *Mort* case above.

Child Support Agency

In 1991 Parliament passed the Child Support Act which established the Child Support Agency as a body to take over from the courts the responsibility for proceeding against absent parents for maintenance payments to support children. The fact that magistrates cannot challenge the Agency's maintenance formula may mean that the work of the agency will bring few Convention points to the courts even though the agency needs to obtain a liability order from the court before it can proceed to take some enforcement measures.

However the Agency itself may be challenged on the basis that it's activities infringe Article 6. Once the magistrates' court has made a liability order, distress can be used to collect the debt and ultimately imprisonment can be ordered by a court. To that extent, CSA cases may attract Convention issues on the basis of the principles already outlined.

ORDERS 'OTHER THAN FOR THE PAYMENT OF MONEY'

By way of somewhat strange terminology, section 63 Magistrates' Courts Act 1980 gives courts certain powers when enforcing their own orders 'other than for the payment of money', i.e. the court can impose a fine not exceeding £5,000 or commit to custody for up to two months (which may be suspended on terms). In practice, a common request for courts to use section 63 relates to the enforcement of a contact order (i.e. allowing contact between parents and children) where the latter do not live with the former.

Enforcement of contact has always been inherently problematic for courts and a large body of case law has developed. In practice, courts tend to avoid strict interpretation of section 63. This is on the basis that committing the custodial parent will do nothing for the welfare of a child. However, Article 8 demands respect for family life—and the case of *Hokkanen v. Finland* (1996) 1 FLR 289 has emphasised that the state has a *positive obligation* to ensure that this right is respected. In that case a national court had granted access to the applicant to see his child who was looked after by grandparents. The grandparents refused access and the court and authorities, in effect, refused to enforce the order. The applicant's claim under Article 8 was upheld. Changes in the way contact orders are enforced seem likely after the 1998 Act is in force.

Occupation orders

Courts may also face submissions under article 8 (right to a family life) and/or the First Protocol, Article 1 (protection of possessions) when enforcing occupation orders made under Part IV Family Law Act 1996. However, the nature of these orders makes it likely that these issues will have been equally relevant at the time when the original order was made. In most case, therefore, arguments concerning the Convention are likely to have been anticipated and dealt with at that time. However orders made prior to 2 October 2000 but enforced after that date could be more likely to attract Convention-based arguments.

Chapter 8: The Convention and Enforcement

Some key points:

- this chapter is about the significant role that the Convention will play in relation to the enforcement process

- courts should be careful to assess whether proceedings are *criminal* or *civil* according to the Convention and to act accordingly

- the principal of *proportionality* should always be adhered to—and there may be situations in which due to this principle or other Convention considerations enforcement sanctions authorised by UK law will not be justified under Convention law.

CHAPTER 9

The Convention and Civil Proceedings

Readers are reminded that it is crucial to determine whether proceedings classified as civil in national law will be regarded as such by the Court of Human Rights. The *Benham* case—mentioned in *Chapters 5* and *8*—gives guidance on the criteria the court adopts when making such decisions. If proceedings *are* regarded as criminal then articles 6(2) and (3) (the presumption of innocence and 'extra' minimum standards with respect to the right to a fair trial) will apply. This means, in particular, that the presumption of innocence and the criminal standard of proof will be invoked and legal aid should be available.

COMPLAINTS

In magistrates' courts most civil proceedings are started by 'complaint'[1] and are governed by rule 14 Magistrates Courts Rules 1981. One complaint which magistrates hear regularly is that brought under section 115 Magistrates Courts Act 1980 for someone to be bound over to keep the peace. *In Steel and Others v. UK* 1999 EHRLR 109 the Court held that the concepts of 'breach of the peace' and of 'binding over' are sufficiently precise to comply with the requirement that an interference by the state must be 'prescribed by law'. The applicants were alleging breaches of Articles 10 (freedom of expression) and 11 (freedom of assembly and association).

However in *Joseph Hashman and Wanda Harrup v. United Kingdom* (Application No. 25594/94) the Commission gave the opinion that the concept of binding over to be of good behaviour was itself imprecise and offers little guidance to the person bound over as to the type of conduct which would amount to a breach of an order to keep the peace. The applicants were anti-hunt supporters who blew a horn and shouted at the hounds. The magistrates found there had been no violence or threats of violence and no breach of the peace had occurred or was likely to occur but the defendants behaviour had not been 'good behaviour' and was likely to re-occur. The applicant's appeal against being bound over was dismissed by the Crown Court and legal aid was refused for them to

---

[1] Meaning, in effect, 'application'—a term now often used instead of the word complaint, particularly in family matters. A *complaint* is the civil equivalent of an *information* to start criminal proceedings.

state a case for the opinion of the High Court. The Commission found, in the circumstances, a breach of Article 10 above. Complaints to bind someone over to be of good behaviour are likely to be relegated to history when the Act is implemented. Indeed, it is arguable that they should cease to exist immediately. It may well be that there has already been a shift in some circumstances to using the Protection From Harassment Act 1997 (which creates both criminal offences and civil rights) but it is equally arguable that the term 'harassment' (which is only partially and loosely defined by the 1997 Act) could lead to analogous problems of imprecision and proceedings before the Court.

CRIME AND DISORDER ACT 1998

The Crime and Disorder Act 1998 was the flagship of the New Labour government's first legislative programme. Many commentators believe the objectives of this Act may come into conflict with 'rights brought home' by the Human Rights Act 1998.

Anti-social behaviour orders

Section 1(3) Crime and Disorder Act provides that an application for an anti-social behaviour order shall be way of compliant to the magistrates' court. Section 2(3) makes a similar statement in respect of applications for sex offender orders. If either type of order is made and the defendant thereafter does something that is prohibited by that order he can be sentenced to prison for up to five years.

In its guidance on the Act, the Home Office has emphasised that these proceedings will be *civil* especially as to the standard of proof. It will now be clear to readers that this guidance may prove to be wrong in the context of the Convention. The Court is unlikely to regard proceedings as civil given the ultimate sanction of imprisonment. The effect seems to be that people facing such applications must be entitled to legal aid and the courts may well have to apply the criminal standard of proof, beyond reasonable doubt.

Further consequences may follow. Applications for anti-social behaviour orders may rely for their success on professional witnesses as to the behaviour that gave rise to the application. Some, if not all of this evidence, may contain hearsay (which itself creates additional hazards if such proceedings are *criminal* proceedings: see *Chapter 8*), which is understandable given the possible intimidating effect of some anti-social behaviour making witnesses with first-hand accounts reluctant to speak out against, say, a local 'family from Hell'. However, members of that family also have important rights under the Convention and it must be remembered that a central purpose of human rights law is to prevent the kind of singling out or scapegoating which can lead to a more general abuse of power and state oppression. If the proceedings are indeed criminal—and the *Benham* principle strongly suggest that they are (it is also arguable that they should be so classed on the basis of their inherent nature and the scale of state interference allowed)—there may be difficulties for magistrates' courts under Article 6 if the defendant is not able to call evidence and cross-examine the witnesses against him or her.

But perhaps more fundamentally, there is a question mark against the whole concept of 'anti-social behaviour'. If specific behaviour is a crime in then this can be dealt with under national law relating to individual crimes. If behaviour is not intrinsically criminally, then how can it be dealt with as if it were (as is likely to be demanded in relation to anti-social behaviour orders by the Convention in view of the criminal nature of the penalties)? There is also the issue of uncertainity, or 'no punishment without law' (Article 7).

It has been pointed out by commentators that 'anti-social' is a dangerously subjective concept which depends on the standpoint of the observer and is open to misuse, especially via discrimination at the behest of the authorities, bringing further problems with Convention rights such as Article 14 (freedom from discrimination), Article 8 (right to respect for private life) and Article 9 (freedom of thought, conscience and religion). Whatever, such applications will require courts to balance the rights of individuals against the rights of society as a whole and this goes to the heart of the judicial oath, the duty to do right to all manner of people. If the court is not satisfied that it can make such an order without contravening the Convention, then the court must dismiss the application.

LICENSING MATTERS

Licensing work—sometimes described as 'administrative'—in relation to sales of alcohol accounts for some two per cent of the workload of magistrates' courts, whether conducted before the licensing committee at transfer sessions or before the ordinary bench (e.g. applications for extensions of hours, occasional licences and protection orders).

The Licensing Act 1964 as amended establishes the procedures to be followed both by applicants and magistrates themselves. Issues which might become relevant when the 1998 Act is in force are as follows:

- a point which some licensing lawyers have already raised relates to the composition of the Crown Court when hearing licensing appeals from magistrates. That court must have a judge and four magistrates, two of whom are from the licensing committee whose decision is the subject of the appeal. Although these two magistrates will not have adjudicated at the original hearing, can such a tribunal really be regarded as impartial for the purposes of Article 6?

- a major issue is the power of licensing justices to revoke existing licences either at their own instigation or upon an application by someone else. This power is contained in section 20A of the 1964 Act. Licences now run for three years and Parliament felt the committee should be able to consider revocation during the lifetime of a licence on specified grounds. However, the power seems to conflict with ordinary rules of natural justice, including the rule that no one can be a judge in their own cause. As the licensing committee is a public authority it must act compatibly with the Convention. The situation where magistrates attempt to revoke a licence of their own motion is therefore likely to be in conflict with Article 6 (right to a fair trial). It is arguable that licensing committees should therefore refrain from considering revocation other than upon application by someone else.

Licensing justices can also expect to hear arguments based on Article 8 (respect for family life) or on the First Protocol, Article 1 (protection of property). Many licensees live on the licensed premises and the case of *Halford v. UK* (1997) 24 EHRR 523 shows that someone's place of work, especially if it is in an office, is capable of attracting the protection of Article 8.

People living near licensed premises may also raise Article 8 arguments claiming that their quality of life is affected adversely by the noise or nuisance from the premises. Again this is an issue which a court must consider as a public authority, but individuals are not directly required to respect these rights unless and until a court orders them to do so.

Returning to revocation issues by way of an example a licensee might argue that revocation is not in the public interest and that he should be able to enjoy peaceful possession of his place of work—which may also be his residence. Conversely, objectors to the licence are likely to argue that the continued existence of the licence infringes, among other things, their First Protocol, Article 1 rights (protection of property)—i.e. if they live nearby and are affected by the noise and nuisance. They will argue that the licensee cannot exercise his Convention rights at the expense of theirs. Given that many of the Convention rights are qualified and therefore require a balance to be struck between the rights of an individual and those of other people it is inevitable that revocation proceedings will raise Convention points—as may applications for new licences.

FAMILY MATTERS

The specialist jurisdiction of the family proceedings court is also part of the civil jurisdiction of the magistrates' court and this is dealt with separately in *Chapter 6*. The broad principles discussed in that chapter are equally applicable here and serve to reinforce the points made above.

Chapter 9: The Convention and Civil Proceedings

Some key points:

- this chapter is about identifying some of the areas of civil proceedings and similar responsibilities where the Convention is likely to have an impact

- it is also about recognising the classification of proceedings as *civil* or *criminal* and the kind of arguments that may well be raised in court at an early stage after the Human Rights Act comes into force in October 2000. The chapter also indicates (with special reference to 'anti-social behaviour') why courts should not be dismissive of such arguments, especially when raised by seemingly marginalised groups or individuals

- above all, the chapter is about 'bringing rights and justice home' in civil proceedings and in relation to similar judicial responsibilities, whether balancing the rights of citizens against those of the state and a community or with those of other citizens.

CHAPTER 10

The Convention and the Courtroom

As emphasised in earlier chapters, section 6 Human Rights Act 1998 makes the court a 'public authority' and because of this it is unlawful for a court or court official to act in a way which is incompatible with a Convention right. The Act places a *positive* duty on courts to ensure that human rights are respected. Article 14 of the Convention also provides for the rights and freedoms in the Convention to be enjoyed equally by all people.

This appears to go some way beyond the principles of natural justice and fairness which are already basic to day-to-day decision-making and training (and which still continue if, in future, they will be reinforced and somewhat enhanced). The effect of section 6 and Article 14 (prohibition of discrimination) are such that the court is required not merely to determine Convention issues raised by a court user, but also to take positive action, of its own volition, to ensure that the human rights of *all* court users are not infringed either by the court or by other court users. This will on occasion mean that the court must be pro-active and it may need to 'step into the arena' by interrupting (or even halting the progress of a case) to ensure compliance with Convention rights.

INTERPRETERS

The general right to a fair trial in Article 6 requires that a defendant must be able to fully participate in the hearing. It is also stated in Article 6(3)(e) that in criminal proceedings the defendant has the right to the assistance of an interpreter, free of charge, if he or she cannot understand or speak the language used in court.

The right is unconditional. Once a request is made for assistance it must be complied with. As already indicated, as a public authority the court is under a duty to protect the Convention rights of all court users. If therefore, it becomes apparent that the defendant (or maybe the defendant's parents in the youth court) are having difficulty following the proceedings then the court must act of its own initiative to provide assistance. The assistance—which may involve a foreign language interpreter or a sign language interpreter—must be provided free of charge irrespective of the defendant's means and cannot be recovered following conviction by an order for costs against the defendant.

As indicated, this right to the free assistance of an interpreter is restricted to criminal proceedings. There currently exists no such absolute right in civil proceedings. Proceedings, e.g. for non-compliance with a court order which carry a threat of imprisonment would be classed as criminal and would thus require the provision of a free interpreter, if needed.[1]

PROVISION OF FACILITIES AND TIME

As part of the fair trial guarantee provided by the Convention, Article 6(3)(b) states that everyone charged with a criminal offence shall 'have adequate time and facilities for the preparation of his defence'. The overriding aim of this provision is to ensure that the defendant is not at a disadvantage as against the prosecutor—and as such it links to the general principle of *equality of arms* (see *Chapter 2*). In one case decided by the Court (*X v. Austria* 1979 15 DR 160) a period of ten working days to prepare for trial was held to be sufficient. However, the need to consider each case on its merits means that only by listening to the representations made will courts be able to determine what period of adjournment, if any, is justified.

The provisions of the Crime and Disorder Act 1998 which require defendants to be bailed to the next available court and timetables to be set, and government initiatives to reduce delay and monitor performance, all put pressure on courts to progress matters and may appear to conflict with the requirement to allow adequate time for the defendant to prepare for trial. However, in themselves, these matters ought not to give rise to challenges—provided that courts continue to fully determine each case individually on its merits. The inflexible application of a bench norm would almost certainly breach a defendant's human rights, if in his or her particular case the time allowed turned out to be insufficient for proper preparation.

DETENTION CONDITIONS

Article 3 provides that 'no-one shall be subjected to torture or degrading treatment or punishment'. The protection offered by Article 3 is one to which everyone is entitled and the fact that a defendant may be lawfully detained by an order of a court is irrelevant. As a public authority, the court must not only ensure that it is not itself responsible for a breach of

---

[1] See the discussion in *Chapter 9*: the meaning of criminal proceedings is wider than that to which UK courts have been accustomed. It must also be remembered that the Court of Human Rights will apply its own rules when determining whether or not a matter is criminal or civil.

Article 3 but must also ensure that other people do not breach the Article so far as this could result from the actions of the court. The Court has further defined 'degrading treatment' as that which arouses in the victim a feeling of fear, anguish and inferiority. The most likely ways in which claims under Article 3 will be made in relation to court proceeding are:

- handcuffing in court (though not simply of itself now: see p.35)

- conditions in the cells, and

- the transporting of prisoners in cellular vans.

It is also arguable, e.g. that poor positioning of the defendant (as in some large/older courtrooms) so that he or she cannot participate effectively and on equal terms could be a source of challenge on general principles already outlined. However, the Court has indicated that a 'minimum level of severity' must be reached before the state can be said to be in breach of Article 3. In *Delazarus v. UK* Appl. 17525 (16 February 1993) the Commission declared that locking prisoners in their cells for 23 hours a day, in conditions criticised by HM Chief Inspector of Prisons, was not a breach of Article 3. Provided accommodation is of a reasonable standard, people are not handcuffed unjustifiably or kept in vans for excessive periods courts should not be found to have breached Article 3.

However, one area that may cause difficulty is the need to provide private and confidential accommodation in which the defendant may communicate with his lawyer. Whilst not specifically referred to in the Convention, the Court has interpreted Article 6(3) as giving a right to private lawyer/client communication as a basic requirement of a fair trial. Again, courts must take positive action to protect rights. Once a defendant objects to speaking to his or her legal representative in the presence of other prisoners or a prison escort, personal and private facilities must be provided.

IMPARTIALITY AND BIAS

The right to a fair trial contained in Article 6 is one of the most fundamental rights conferred by the Convention. The Article requires a hearing 'by an independent and impartial tribunal'. In the United Kingdom the courts are sufficiently separated from both the legislature and the executive so as not to give cause for concern with regard to independence (although, indicative of the wide scope of Convention rights, at the time of writing an office analogous to that of Lord Chancellor—as a judge, head of the judiciary and a member of the Cabinet—is itself under challenge in Europe from the Channel Islands).

Impartiality

With regard to impartiality, the Court places equal importance on the *appearance* of impartiality as it does on *actual* impartiality; justice must not only be done but must also be seen to be done. As at present—under the rules of natural justice—great care will have to be taken to ensure that a bench of magistrates dealing with a trial has no prior knowledge of facts which may influence the decision or cause the defendant to question the court's impartiality. Knowledge of previous convictions is an obvious example. Magistrates who have heard a bail application during which the defendant's previous convictions were referred to should not sit on the trial. Each case must be looked at individually. In *Pullar v. UK* 1006 22 EHRR 391 the Court held that the fact that one of the jury was employed by a prosecution witness did not mean that the trial was unfair. However detailed personal knowledge of the defendant or his case would obviously be sufficient to raise the appearance of bias.

In *Brown v. UK* 1985 8 EHRR 273 the Commission rejected a complaint based on a trial judge having previously granted an injunction in the case. The fact that a member of the bench has determined a preliminary point or dealt with some earlier part of the process which does not involve 'tainted' information (such, perhaps, as granting a search warrant which ultimately led to the arrest of the defendant) should not cause a problem so long as the degree or nature of any advance knowledge is not such as to raise the issue of bias. If in doubt, it is best to err on the side of caution—by making the parties aware of the connection, avoiding any form of pressure on the defence 'not to cause a fuss' and acting on any objection raised.

The role of the court clerk/legal adviser

The role of the court legal adviser at various stages of proceedings may itself give rise to challenge. Firstly, giving advice in the privacy of the retiring room denies the defendant the opportunity to participate by challenging the accuracy of the adviser's legal opinion or the nature and extent of his or her involvement in the decision-making process. The exclusion of prosecutor, defendant and/or defence lawyer from this important aspect of the criminal process may be sufficient to render the trial proceedings unfair. Giving advice in open court would remove the perception that the clerk may be 'misleading' the magistrates or indeed is influencing factual decision-making (something which conflicts with his or her responsibilities). In *Gregory v. UK* (1997) 25 EHRR 577 the Court held that the secrecy of jury deliberations was *not* a ground for declaring a trial unfair. However, in the Crown Court, only those charged with making the decision about guilt or innocence are present and there are rules which ensure 'open' communication with the judge.

Giving all advice in open court also averts any potential challenge based on the fact that the same legal adviser—having assisted a differently constituted bench of magistrates at an earlier stage of a case—might pass on information to a future bench dealing with the matter, or allow his or her advice to be affected by prior knowledge of what has occurred.

FACTS AND REASONS FOR DECISIONS

It is an integral part of a fair and impartial hearing that parties are provided with reasons for the court's judgement. A main reason for this is that it is impossible for a defendant to effectively challenge a decision of a court if he or she is given no explanation and is unaware of the basis upon which it was made. Magistrates are already required by national law to give reasons in a range of situations, such as when refusing bail, attaching conditions to bail or imposing a custodial sentence.

The need to give reasons will in future occur at *every* stage of the proceedings and with regard to all decisions. However, the nature of the explanation will vary with the kind of decision in question. In the case of a contested application for an adjournment the reasons could be quite short, and simply indicate briefly what exactly persuaded the court to decide one way rather than another. In the case of a verdict the reasons would be much fuller, any point which was highly contested during the trial demanding specific attention and explanation. As always, reasons must be grounded in the facts as found by the court.

Giving reasons (which courts should always have for their decisions in any event) is a positive discipline and one very much aided by structured decision-making. It should not add significantly to the length of court hearings where the issues are straightforward. However, depending on existing local practice, decisions on guilt or innocence may require more time if key facts are to be noted, a structured approach applied and sound and matching reasons are to be formulated.

PRESS DIRECTIONS

The press and other media are always keen to publish details of court proceedings, especially concerning the 'rich or famous', while many court users would rather nothing appeared at all. Against the background of the general principle of open court (next section) and the longstanding practice of open reporting, courts currently have power to restrict the publication of some or all of the details of a case in specified circumstances. In future, the media may try to challenge restriction orders on the basis that they breach Article 10 (right to freedom of expression, which includes a right to impart information and ideas).

This freedom is, however, *qualified* in that the state may by legislation deemed necessary in a democratic society restrict the right in order to achieve certain aims set out in Article 10(2)—which include national security, the prevention of crime and the protection of the rights and freedoms of other people.

Directions to the press made under section 39 Children and Young Persons Act 1933 not to publish details which would lead to the identification of any child involved in the proceedings would appear to be within the scope of the exception (and publication could also be argued as an interference with privacy in the sense that a child may be far more vulnerable than an adult to the possibly 'morbid' or dubious attentions of members of the general public). As the present power is clearly prescribed by law the question of necessity in a democratic society must be addressed. If a pressing social need exists and the measure goes no further than is necessary to meet that need then the restriction will be deemed necessary in a democratic society. There is likely to be little argument that the non-identification of children represents a pressing social need. A direction under Section 39 goes no further than is necessary to achieve that aim and would therefore seem to satisfy Article 10. The fact that it may give the defendant protection as a result should be regarded as irrelevant.

Open court—Public hearings and public judgements
The right of the public and the media to attend court hearings is an important aspect of ensuring that proceedings are conducted fairly as required by Article 6. However, the right of the public and the media to be present during a trial is qualified. The right to be present when judgement is pronounced is similarly qualified.

Courts have a general discretion to exclude the media and the public from all or part of the proceedings

> in the interests of morals, public order or national security in a democratic society, where the interests of juveniles or the protection of the private life of the parties so require or to the extent that the court considers it strictly necessary in special circumstance where publicity would prejudice the interests of justice.

In order to give public judgment in a case, say, involving child witnesses who have given sensitive evidence in private—and without causing unnecessary further distress or anxiety—it would seem that any court choosing to give public judgement about such matters should avoid naming the children concerned or adopt the practice of referring to children by the initial of their name, i.e. R for Robert, S for Sarah etc. (as the Court often does, and the High Court in England and Wales).

There currently exist a number of situations where the public are excluded as a matter of course as a result of national legislation such as the blanket ban which exists in family courts (the situation regarding youth courts is dealt with in *Chapter 11*). The court also has power to sit in camera when hearing certain proceedings, e.g. an application by the police for a warrant of extended detention pre-charge.

Section 45 Police and Criminal Evidence Act 1984 provides that when hearing applications made by the police for warrants to further detain suspects the public and press are excluded from the hearing. As stated, Article 6 provides a list of exceptions where exclusion is justified, the relevant proviso which appears to apply here would be that publicity would prejudice the interests of justice by hampering a criminal investigation into a serious offence.

It is also possible for a court to sit in *camera* on grounds of national security, a conclusion which—like others in this particular area of procedure as overlaid by Convention rights—the court must arrive at judicially. It may similarly exclude 'materials' from being used in a case on the same basis, such as 'Top Secret' documents and records. Such action—in practice a rarity—would be directly covered by the words of Article 6 of the Convention.

Chapter 10: The Convention and the Courtroom

Some key points:

- this chapter is about separating out the role of the court and its legal adviser to ensure that the court process is thoroughly impartial and independent —and seen to be such

- it is also about transparency and openness in the decision-making process by sitting and/or giving judgement in open court unless there are proper and valid reasons to do otherwise, and giving reasoned judgements and explanations at all stages of the court process—so that the parties and public can understand what is happening and see that the trial (and thus the processes of justice generally) are fair

- giving reasons and structured-decision making reinforce one another

- courts must deal with individuals as individuals in the enjoyment of their rights, without discrimination—and make each and every decision on its individual merits.

CHAPTER 11

Human Rights and the Youth Court

As explained in *Chapter 1*, the incorporation of Convention rights into UK national law will have a significant impact on current practices and procedures. The overall effects of the Human Rights Act 1998 in magistrates' courts will be mirrored across the full range of powers and procedures of the youth court. In addition, the special restrictions which apply to youth courts and the different types of sentence available will all need to be considered with regard to the Convention rights discussed in earlier chapters. This chapter considers the effect of the Convention on matters relating solely to the youth court and also the way that the general Convention rights will apply there.

ISSUES OF PARTICULAR RELEVANCE

Private hearings

As outlined in the previous chapter, Article 6 (right to a fair trial) provides that everyone 'is entitled to a fair and public hearing' and that 'judgement shall be pronounced publicly'. The requirement relating to *trials* is subject to the proviso that both the press and public may be excluded 'where the interests of juveniles so requires'. The requirement relating to pronouncement of *judgement* is also qualified (see *Chapter 10*).

In youth courts the public are excluded by virtue of section 47 Children and Young Persons Act 1933. This exclusion from the trial, which is clearly prescribed by law for the benefit of the young people involved, is unlikely in itself to cause problems. However, it can be noted that youth courts do have a discretion to admit people other than those entitled to attend and that the government has expressed itself as committed to a greater degree of openness:

> The present government is committed to a wide-ranging programme for reform of the youth justice system and this includes as one of its objectives greater openness in youth court proceedings. It believes that youth courts should make full use of their wide discretion concerning who can attend proceedings. It is also encouraging the removal of the concept that victims often feel they are prevented from attending court to witness proceedings and therefore have no opportunity to understand decisions that are made or

the consequences of these. The government considers it important that victims and the public have confidence in the outcome of proceedings.[1]

The fact that the public are not currently entitled to enter a youth court *to hear judgement pronounced* may give rise to challenge. In *Preto v. Italy* 1983 6 EHRR 182 this right was held to require judgement to be read in open court as well as there being public availability of the outcome. However, the Court stated that the form of publicity of a judgement had to be assessed in the light of the special features of the proceedings being considered and with regard to the purpose of Article 6(1). It is likely that the judgement in a youth court being made in a courtroom with all the parties present and press (if not the public) entitled to attend would be held sufficient when the interests of the young people involved are taken into account. The primary purpose of Article 6(1) is that the defendant should be aware of the judgement against him. However, it should perhaps be re-emphasised that, as indicated in *Chapter 1*, the Convention is about *minimum* standards and a more flexible approach such as that proposed by government would appear to go some way towards ensuring that the new requirements are met.

Press restrictions

As outlined in *Chapter 10*, there is normally free access to the press and other media and freedom to report whatever they wish. Whilst there is such access to the youth court, when publishing reports of proceedings of that court reporters are prohibited from:

> . . . publishing the name, address or school of any child or young person involved in the proceedings or any particulars likely to lead to the identification of the child or young person. (Section 49 Children and Young Persons Act 1933).

This may again lead to a challenge under Article 10 (freedom of expression). The right to 'receive and impart information' is regarded by Strasbourg as being particularly important. However, Article 10 expressly provides that the exercise of the freedoms in Article 10 carries with it duties and responsibilities which may, therefore, result in restrictions 'prescribed by law and . . . necessary in a democratic society'. When the right to report is balanced against the interests of the child and his or her Article 8 rights to a private life and the limited restrictions on

---

[1] *Introduction to Youth Justice,* Winston Gordon, Philip Cuddy and Jonathan Black, Waterside Press, 1999. The authors instance the admission to the youth court of representatives of a community which has been the subject of criminal offending.

publication—not on reporting the outcome—together with a statutory discretion to lift the restriction to avoid injustice this might well be deemed proportionate.

Parental bind-overs

Youth courts have power (in the case of a defendant under the age of 16 normally a *duty*), to order the parent or guardian to enter into a recognizance to take proper care of and exercise proper control over a minor convicted of a criminal offence. The parent is required to consent or face a fine of up to £1,000 for any unreasonable refusal.

Article 7 prohibits punishment without lawful authority. This is often concerned with the introduction of more stringent retrospective penalties or to the retrospective criminalisation of particular conduct. However, the Court has interpreted this right as embodying the principal of legal certainty. Thus the law is required to spell out in clear terms exactly what behaviour is permitted or prohibited. Problems with parental bind-overs are almost certain to arise at the enforcement stage. Parents may seek to challenge the forfeiture of a recognizance on the grounds that, when originally made, the order was not sufficiently clear as to the exact action which they had to take to avoid forfeiture.

The position is not unlike that in relation to binding over discussed in *Chapter 9* and the case of *Joseph Hashman and Wanda Harrup v. UK* (Application No. 25594/94) could be relevant to this issue also. The decision by the Commission that the concept of 'good behaviour' breached Article 10 because of its vagueness and uncertainty would seem to support an argument that being bound over to keep control of children is also too vague.

Orders made under the Crime and Disorder Act 1998

Parenting orders

Where a child or young person is convicted of an offence, or made subject of an anti-social behaviour order (itself quite problematic: see *Chapter 9*), a sex offender order or a child safety order the court may make a 'parenting order'—provided that it is satisfied that the making of such an order would be desirable in the interests of preventing further offending by the juvenile or any repetition of the conduct which led to the making of the order. In the case of a person under the age of 16 the court is under a *duty* to make the parenting order if satisfied that one of the specified reasons for making it exists. If not so satisfied, then the court must state this and give reasons in support of that conclusion. Such an order requires the parent to:

- comply with such requirements as are specified for a period of up to 12 months; and
- attend counselling or guidance sessions as required by the supervising officer.

The court must obtain and consider information about the family circumstances and the likely effect of the order, and explain to the parent the effect of the order and the consequences of breach, before making an order.

Challenges to parenting orders are likely to be made on two grounds. Firstly, that the order itself breaches the parent's right to respect for private and family life provided for by Article 8. When making parenting orders courts are required so far as possible to avoid any conflict or interference with a parent's religious beliefs, work or education. If this requirement is complied with the likelihood of challenges will be reduced. However, challenges may still be made, e.g. on the ground that compliance with the order is adversely affecting a parent's ability to care for other children of the family. The right to respect to private and family life is *qualified* in that the state may intervene so long as the interference is prescribed by law and is necessary in a democratic society 'for the prevention of disorder or crime or for the protection of health or morals'. The power to make parenting orders and the circumstances which must exist *are* clearly prescribed. Any challenge is likely to focus on whether the making of an order in the terms specified was necessary in order to achieve one or more legitimate aims of the Convention.

In the past, Strasbourg has determined that national laws designed to protect society in general can and have breached an individual's right to respect for private and family life. In the case of parenting orders only those directly involved with people named in the order will be affected. Provided, therefore, that the court has avoided, so far as practicable, interference with the religious practices, work and education of the parents it seems likely that the impact of the order on such rights will be seen as justified in the light of the protection it offers society in general.

The second way in which such orders may be challenged is by parents facing conviction for failing to comply with a requirement of the order or direction of the responsible officer: on the basis that the requirement alleged to have been breached was not sufficiently clear to enable the parent to be sure what exactly was required—and that it is therefore contrary to the requirement that there shall be 'no punishment without law' (Article 7).

As noted above, Article 7 has been widely interpreted by the Court to include a requirement of certainty. Rather like bail conditions and parental bind-overs, requirements included in parenting orders must be sufficiently clear, so that there is no room whatsoever for Convention arguments based on a later claim of failure to appreciate what was expected. Clearly worded requirements should withstand challenge.

Reparation orders

Reparation orders require a child or young person to make such reparation as is specified in the order up to a maximum of 24 hours. The court is required to avoid, as far as practicable, any conflict with the defendant's religious beliefs, other community orders, education or work. There is no requirement to obtain the consent of the defendant prior to the making of the order. This may lead to to attempts to challenge the order on the grounds that it breaches the prohibition of forced labour provided for by Article 4.

The inclusion of a requirement to obtain the defendant's consent prior to making an order would remove any such objection but would limit the sentencing power of the court. Anyone consenting to such an order who has the benefit of legal advice is, in any event, unlikely to be able to make a successful claim alleging a breach of Article 4 at a later date. See also the earlier general discussion on this point in *Chapter 5*.

The Crime and Disorder Act 1998 requires that when dealing with a juvenile the court must give reasons for not making a reparation order in circumstances where it has power to do so. Once the Human Rights Act 1998 is implemented the court will be required to give reasons when making *or* declining to make any order—as pointed out in *Chapter 9*.

Action plan orders

If on conviction of a criminal offence the youth court is of the opinion that an 'action plan order' is desirable in the interests of securing the rehabilitation of the defendant or of preventing the commission of further offences by him/her, the defendant may be required:

- for a period of three months to comply with an action plan: a series of requirements with regard to his or her actions and whereabouts;

- to be under the supervision of a responsible officer; and

- to comply with any direction given by that officer with a view to the implementation of the plan.

As with reparation orders, the court is required, as far as is practicable, to avoid any conflict with the offender's religious beliefs, other community orders, occupation or education. The consent of the defendant is not required. A requirements which may be included in an action plan order could be one to make reparation. This could lead to a challenge under Article 4 on the basis outlined in the last section. Obtaining the defendant's consent would appear to solve this problem but in doing so it also limits the sentencing options which the court can impose at will.

The list of requirements that may be included in action plan orders are such that the court has wide powers to restrict the defendant's freedom by requiring him or her to act in a particular way. Even if the court considers the defendant's specific commitments (as required by the Crime and Disorder Act 1998), there is still the possibility of a claim that the order interferes with the defendant's right to respect for private and family life as provided by for by Article 8, and that it is disproportionate. The fact that reports will have been considered prior to making an order should reduce the incidence of inadvertent conflicts with the defendant's other commitments. As with parenting orders, when the benefits to society in general are weighed against the effect a restrictive order will have on a small number of people, balanced restrictions are likely to be held to be justified. Courts must ensure that any requirements are appropriate and proportionate in all the circumstances. Any draconian or unduly restrictive requirement may be viewed as a breach of Article 8 above.

SPECIAL EFFECTS IN THE YOUTH COURT

The rights provided for by Articles 5 (right to liberty and security), 6 (right to a fair trial), 7 (no punishment without law) and 8 (right to respect for private and family life) and others which apply to people in the adult court will apply equally to the defendant and his or her parents in the youth court. But they may often have a special effect. For example, when dealing with points raised under Article 6 the youth court will need to have regard to the defendant's age, and when deciding whether the defendant's rights have been breached and whether the state's actions were proportionate, the court will need to have regard to the age and understanding of the person concerned.

Chapter 11: The Convention and the Youth Court

Some key points:

- this chapter is about protecting the rights of juveniles (and their parents) by ensuring that they are dealt with fairly with regard to their age and possible individual vulnerability

- it is also is about taking care to ensure that conditions or requirements in orders made in the youth court are clear and precise and always ensuring that orders made or instructions given by the court are never vague, imprecise or uncertain, taking full account of the age range dealt with by the court

- above all, it is about 'bringing rights and justice home' in the youth court.

Appendix I

The Human Rights Act 1998

Appendix I: The Human Rights Act 1998

This appendix sets out the main provisions of the 1998 Act leaving out those lesser parts which are not central to an understanding of the provisions. The provisions of Schedule 1 to the Act (the Articles and The First Protocol) are reproduced in full in *Chapter 3* (apart from The Sixth Protocol: Abolition of the death penalty); and the broad effect of Schedule 3 (derogations and reservations) is also explained there. For this reason, those provisions are not reproduced below and neither is Schedule 4, 'Judicial Pensions'.

Human Rights Act 1998

1998 CHAPTER 42

An Act to give further effect to rights and freedoms guaranteed under the European Convention on Human Rights; to make provision with respect to holders of certain judicial offices who become judges of the European Court of Human Rights; and for connected purposes. [9th November 1998]

BE IT ENACTED by the Queen's most Excellent Majesty, by and with the advice and consent of the Lords Spiritual and Temporal, and Commons, in this present Parliament assembled, and by the authority of the same, as follows: —

Introduction

The Convention rights
1.(1) In this Act "the Convention rights" means the rights and fundamental freedoms set out in —
  (a) Articles 2 to 12 and 14 of the Convention,
  (b) Articles 1 to 3 of the First Protocol, and
  (c) Articles 1 and 2 of the Sixth Protocol,
as read with Articles 16 to 18 of the Convention.

(2) Those Articles are to have effect for the purposes of this Act subject to any designated derogation or reservation (as to which see sections 14 and 15).

(3) The Articles are set out in Schedule 1.

(4) The Secretary of State may by order make such amendments to this Act as he considers appropriate to reflect the effect, in relation to the United Kingdom, of a protocol.

(5) In subsection (4) "protocol" means a protocol to the Convention —
  (a) which the United Kingdom has ratified; or
  (b) which the United Kingdom has signed with a view to ratification.

(6) No amendment may be made by an order under subsection (4) so as to come into force before the protocol concerned is in force in relation to the United Kingdom.

Interpretation of Convention rights

2.(1) A court or tribunal determining a question which has arisen in connection with a Convention right must take into account any —

(a) judgment, decision, declaration or advisory opinion of the European Court of Human Rights,

(b) opinion of the Commission given in a report adopted under Article 31 of the Convention,

(c) decision of the Commission in connection with Article 26 or 27(2) of the Convention, or

(d) decision of the Committee of Ministers taken under Article 46 of the Convention,

whenever made or given, so far as, in the opinion of the court or tribunal, it is relevant to the proceedings in which that question has arisen.

(2) Evidence of any judgment, decision, declaration or opinion of which account may have to be taken under this section is to be given in proceedings before any court or tribunal in such manner as may be provided by rules.

(3) In this section "rules" means rules of court or, in the case of proceedings before a tribunal, rules made for the purposes of this section —

(a) by the Lord Chancellor or the Secretary of State, in relation to any proceedings outside Scotland;

(b) by the Secretary of State, in relation to proceedings in Scotland; or

(c) by a Northern Ireland department, in relation to proceedings before a tribunal in Northern Ireland —

(i) which deals with transferred matters; and

(ii) for which no rules made under paragraph (a) are in force.

Legislation

Interpretation of legislation

3. — (1) SO far as it is possible to do so, primary legislation and subordinate legislation must be read and given effect in a way which is compatible with the Convention rights.

(2) This section —

(a) applies to primary legislation and subordinate legislation whenever enacted;

(b) does not affect the validity, continuing operation or enforcement of any incompatible primary legislation; and

(c) does not affect the validity, continuing operation or enforcement of any incompatible subordinate legislation if (disregarding any possibility of revocation) primary legislation prevents removal of the incompatibility.

Declaration of incompatibility

4. — (1) Subsection (2) applies in any proceedings in which a court determines whether a provision of primary legislation is compatible with a Convention right.

(2) If the court is satisfied that the provision is incompatible with a Convention right, it may make a declaration of incompatibility.

(3) Subsection (4) applies in any proceedings in which a court determines whether a provision of subordinate legislation, made in the exercise of a power conferred by primary legislation, is compatible with a Convention right.

(4) If the court is satisfied —
(a) that the provision is incompatible with a Convention right, and
(h) that (disregarding any possibility of revocation) the primary legislation concerned prevents removal of the incompatibility,
it may make a declaration of that incompatibility.

(5) In this section "court" means —
(a) the House of Lords;
(b) the Judicial Committee of the Privy Council;
(c) the Courts-Martial Appeal Court;
(d) in Scotland, the High Court of Justiciary sitting otherwise than as a trial court or the Court of Session;
(e) in England and Wales or Northern Ireland, the High Court or the Court of Appeal.

(6) A declaration under this section ("a declaration of incompatibility") —
(a) does not affect the validity, continuing operation or enforcement of the provision in respect of which it is given; and
(b) is not binding on the parties to the proceedings in which it is made.

Right of Crown to intervene

5. — (1) Where a court is considering whether to make a declaration of incompatibility, the Crown is entitled to notice in accordance with rules of court.

(2) In any case to which subsection (1) applies —
(a) a Minister of the Crown (or a person nominated by him),
(b) a member of the Scottish Executive,
(c) a Northern Ireland Minister,
(d) a Northern Ireland department,
is entitled, on giving notice in accordance with rules of court, to be joined as a party to the proceedings.

(3) Notice under subsection (2) may be given at any time during the proceedings.

(4) A person who has been made a party to criminal proceedings (other than in Scotland) as the result of a notice under subsection (2) may, with leave, appeal to the House of Lords against any declaration of incompatibility made in the proceedings.

(5) In subsection (4) —

"criminal proceedings" includes all proceedings before the Courts-Martial Appeal Court; and

"leave" means leave granted by the court making the declaration of incompatibility or by the House of Lords.

Public authorities

Acts of public authorities

6. — (1) It is unlawful for a public authority to act in a way which is incompatible with a Convention right.

(2) Subsection (1) does not apply to an act if —

(a) as the result of one or more provisions of primary legislation, the authority could not have acted differently; or

(b) in the case of one or more provisions of, or made under, primary legislation which cannot be read or given effect in a way which is compatible with the Convention rights, the authority was acting so as to give effect to or enforce those provisions.

(3) In this section "public authority" includes —

(a) a court or tribunal, and

(b) any person certain of whose functions are functions of a public nature,
but does not include either House of Parliament or a person exercising functions in connection with proceedings in Parliament.

(4) In subsection (3) "Parliament" does not include the House of Lords in its judicial capacity.

(5) In relation to a particular act, a person is not a public authority by virtue only of subsection (3)(b) if the nature of the act is private.

(6) "An act" includes a failure to act but does not include a failure to —

(a) introduce in, or lay before, Parliament a proposal for legislation; or

(b) make any primary legislation or remedial order.

Proceedings

7. — (1) A person who claims that a public authority has acted (or proposes to act) in a way which is made unlawful by section 6(1) may —

(a) bring proceedings against the authority under this Act in the appropriate court or tribunal, or

(b) rely on the Convention right or rights concerned in any legal proceedings, but only if he is (or would be) a victim of the unlawful act.

(2) In subsection (1)(a) "appropriate court or tribunal" means such court or tribunal as may be determined in accordance with rules; and proceedings against an authority include a counterclaim or similar proceeding.

(3) If the proceedings are brought on an application for judicial review, the applicant is to be taken to have a sufficient interest in relation to the unlawful act only if he is, or would be, a victim of that act.

(4) If the proceedings are made by way of a petition for judicial review in Scotland, the applicant shall be taken to have title and interest to sue in relation to the unlawful act only if he is, or would be, a victim of that act.

(5) Proceedings under subsection (1)(a) must be brought before the end of —
(a) the period of one year beginning with the date on which the act complained of took place; or
(b) such longer period as the court or tribunal considers equitable having regard to all the circumstances,
but that is subject to any rule imposing a stricter time limit in relation to the procedure in question.

(6) In subsection (1)(b) "legal proceedings" includes —
(a) proceedings brought by or at the instigation of a public authority; and
(b) an appeal against the decision of a court or tribunal.

(7) For the purposes of this section, a person is a victim of an unlawful act only if he would be a victim for the purposes of Article 34 of the Convention if proceedings were brought in the European Court of Human Rights in respect of that act.

(8) Nothing in this Act creates a criminal offence.

(9) In this section "rules" means —
(a) in relation to proceedings before a court or tribunal outside Scotland, rules made by the Lord Chancellor or the Secretary of State for the purposes of this section or rules of court,
(b) in relation to proceedings before a court or tribunal in Scotland, rules made by the Secretary of State for those purposes,
(c) in relation to proceedings before a tribunal in Northern Ireland —
(i) which deals with transferred matters; and
(ii) for which no rules made under paragraph (a) are in force,
rules made by a Northern Ireland department for those purposes,
and includes provision made by order under section 1 of the Courts and Legal Services Act 1990.

(10) In making rules, regard must be had to section 9.

(11) The Minister who has power to make rules in relation to a particular tribunal may, to the extent he considers it necessary to ensure that the tribunal can provide an appropriate remedy in relation to an act (or proposed act) of a public authority which is (or would be) unlawful as a result of section 6(1), by order add to —

(a) the relief or remedies which the tribunal may grant; or

(b) the grounds on which it may grant any of them.

(12) An order made under subsection (11) may contain such incidental, supplemental, consequential or transitional provision as the Minister making it considers appropriate.

(13) "The Minister" includes the Northern Ireland department concerned.

Judicial remedies

8. — (1) In relation to any act (or proposed act) of a public authority which the court finds is (or would be) unlawful, it may grant such relief or remedy, or make such order, within its powers as it considers just and appropriate.

(2) But damages may be awarded only by a court which has power to award damages, or to order the payment of compensation, in civil proceedings.

(3) No award of damages is to be made unless, taking account of all the circumstances of the case, including —

(a) any other relief or remedy granted, or order made, in relation to the act in question (by that or any other court), and

(b) the consequences of any decision (of that or any other court) in respect of that act,

the court is satisfied that the award is necessary to afford just satisfaction to the person in whose favour it is made.

(4) In determining —

(a) whether to award damages, or

(b) the amount of an award,

the court must take into account the principles applied by the European Court of Human Rights in relation to the award of compensation under Article 41 of the Convention.

(5) A public authority against which damages are awarded is to be treated —

(a) in Scotland, for the purposes of section 3 of the Law Reform (Miscellaneous Provisions) (Scotland) Act 1940 as if the award were made in an action of damages in which the authority has been found liable in respect of loss or damage to the person to whom the award is made;

(b) for the purposes of the Civil Liability (Contribution) Act 1978 as liable in respect of damage suffered by the person to whom the award is made.

(6) In this section—

"court" includes a tribunal;

"damages" means damages for an unlawful act of a public authority; and

"unlawful" means unlawful under section 6(1).

Judicial acts

9.(1) Proceedings under section 7(1)(a) in respect of a judicial act may be brought only—

(a) by exercising a right of appeal;

(b) on an application (in Scotland a petition) for judicial review; or

(c) in such other forum as may be prescribed by rules.

(2) That does not affect any rule of law which prevents a court from being the subject of judicial review.

(3) In proceedings under this Act in respect of a judicial act done in good faith, damages may not be awarded otherwise than to compensate a person to the extent required by Article 5(5) of the Convention.

(4) An award of damages permitted by subsection (3) is to be made against the Crown; but no award may be made unless the appropriate person, if not a party to the proceedings, is joined.

(5) In this section—

"appropriate person" means the Minister responsible for the court concerned, or a person or government department nominated by him;

"court" includes a tribunal;

"judge" includes a member of a tribunal, a justice of the peace and a clerk or other officer entitled to exercise the jurisdiction of a court;

"judicial act" means a judicial act of a court and includes an act done on the instructions, or on behalf, of a judge; and

"rules" has the same meaning as in section 7(9).

Remedial action

Power to take remedial action

10(1)—This section applies if—

(a) a provision of legislation has been declared under section 4 to be remedial action. incompatible with a Convention right and, if an appeal lies—

(i) all persons who may appeal have stated in writing that they do not intend to do so;

(ii) the time for bringing an appeal has expired and no appeal has been brought within that time; or

(iii) an appeal brought within that time has been determined or abandoned; or

(b) it appears to a Minister of the Crown or Her Majesty in Council that, having regard to a finding of the European Court of Human Rights made after the coming into force of this section in proceedings against the United

Kingdom, a provision of legislation is incompatible with an obligation of the United Kingdom arising from the Convention.

(2) If a Minister of the Crown considers that there are compelling reasons for proceeding under this section, he may by order make such amendments to the legislation as he considers necessary to remove the incompatibility.

(3) If, in the case of subordinate legislation, a Minister of the Crown considers —

(a) that it is necessary to amend the primary legislation under which the subordinate legislation in question was made, in order to enable the incompatibility to be removed, and

(b) that there are compelling reasons for proceeding under this section,

he may by order make such amendments to the primary legislation as he considers necessary.

(4) This section also applies where the provision in question is in subordinate legislation and has been quashed, or declared invalid, by reason of incompatibility with a Convention right and the Minister proposes to proceed under paragraph 2(b) of Schedule 2.

(5) If the legislation is an Order in Council, the power conferred by subsection (2) or (3) is exercisable by Her Majesty in Council.

(6) In this section "legislation" does not include a Measure of the Church Assembly or of the General Synod of the Church of England.

(7) Schedule 2 makes further provision about remedial orders.

Other rights and proceedings

Safeguard for existing human rights

11. A person's reliance on a Convention right does not restrict —

(a) any other right or freedom conferred on him by or under any law having effect in any part of the United Kingdom; or

(b) his right to make any claim or bring any proceedings which he could make or bring apart from sections 7 to 9.

Freedom of expression

12. — (1) This section applies if a court is considering whether to grant any relief which, if granted, might affect the exercise of the Convention right to freedom of expression.

(2) If the person against whom the application for relief is made ("the respondent") is neither present nor represented, no such relief is to be granted unless the court is satisfied —

(a) that the applicant has taken all practicable steps to notify the respondent; or

(b) that there are compelling reasons why the respondent should not be notified.

(3) No such relief is to be granted so as to restrain publication before trial unless the court is satisfied that the applicant is likely to establish that publication should not be allowed.

(4) The court must have particular regard to the importance of the Convention right to freedom of expression and, where the proceedings relate to material which the respondent claims, or which appears to the court, to be journalistic, literary or artistic material (or to conduct connected with such material), to —
(a) the extent to which —
(i) the material has, or is about to, become available to the public; or
(ii) it is, or would be, in the public interest for the material to be published;
(b) any relevant privacy code.

(5) In this section —
"court" includes a tribunal; and
"relief" includes any remedy or order (other than in criminal proceedings).

Freedom of thought, conscience and religion

13.(1) If a court's determination of any question arising under this Act might affect the exercise by a religious organisation (itself or its members collectively) of the Convention right to freedom of thought, conscience and religion, it must have particular regard to the importance of that right.

(2) In this section "court" includes a tribunal.

Derogations and reservations

Derogations

14. — (1) In this Act "designated derogation" means —
(a) the United Kingdom's derogation from Article 5(3) of the Convention; and
(b) any derogation by the United Kingdom from an Article of the Convention, or of any protocol to the Convention, which is designated for the purposes of this Act in an order made by the Secretary of State.

(2) The derogation referred to in subsection (1)(a) is set out in Part I of Schedule 3.

(3) If a designated derogation is amended or replaced it ceases to be a designated derogation.

(4) But subsection (3) does not prevent the Secretary of State from exercising his power under subsection (1)(b) to make a fresh designation order in respect of the Article concerned.

(5) The Secretary of State must by order make such amendments to Schedule 3 as he considers appropriate to reflect —
(a) any designation order; or
(b) the effect of subsection (3).

(6) A designation order may be made in anticipation of the making by the United Kingdom of a proposed derogation.

Reservations
15.(1) — In this Act "designated reservation" means —
(a) the United Kingdom's reservation to Article 2 of the First Protocol to the Convention; and
(b) any other reservation by the United Kingdom to an Article of the Convention, or of any protocol to the Convention, which is designated for the purposes of this Act in an order made by the Secretary of State.

(2) The text of the reservation referred to in subsection (l)(a) is set out in Part II of Schedule 3.

(3) If a designated reservation is withdrawn wholly or in part it ceases to be a designated reservation.

(4) But subsection (3) does not prevent the Secretary of State from exercising his power under subsection (l)(b) to make a fresh designation order in respect of the Article concerned.

(5) The Secretary of State must by order make such amendments to this Act as he considers appropriate to reflect —
(a) any designation order; or
(b) the effect of subsection (3).

Period for which designated derogations have effect
16.(1) If it has not already been withdrawn by the United Kingdom, a designated derogation ceases to have effect for the purposes of this Act —
(a) in the case of the derogation referred to in section 14(1)(a), at the end of the period of five years beginning with the date on which section 1(2) came into force;
(b) in the case of any other derogation, at the end of the period of five years beginning with the date on which the order designating it was made.

(2) At any time before the period —
(a) fixed by subsection (l)(a) or (b), or
(b) extended by an order under this subsection,
comes to an end, the Secretary of State may by order extend it by a further period of five years.

(3) An order under section 14(1)(b) ceases to have effect at the end of the period for consideration, unless a resolution has been passed by each House approving the order.

(4) Subsection (3) does not affect—

(a) anything done in reliance on the order; or

(b) the power to make a fresh order under section 14(1)(b).

(5) In subsection (3) "period for consideration" means the period of forty days beginning with the day on which the order was made.

(6) In calculating the period for consideration, no account is to be taken of any time during which—

(a) Parliament is dissolved or prorogued; or

(b) both Houses are adjourned for more than four days.

(7) If a designated derogation is withdrawn by the United Kingdom, the Secretary of State must by order make such amendments to this Act as he considers are required to reflect that withdrawal.

Periodic review of designated reservations

17.—(1) The appropriate Minister must review the reservation referred to in section 15(1)(a)—

(a) before the end of the period of five years beginning with the date on which section 1(2) came into force; and

(b) if that designation is still in force, before the end of the period of five years beginning with the date on which-the last report relating to it was laid under subsection (3).

(2) The appropriate Minister must review each of the other designated reservations (if any)—

(a) before the end of the period of five years beginning with the date on which the order designating the reservation first came into force; and

(b) if the designation is still in force, before the end of the period of five years beginning with the date on which the last report relating to it was laid under subsection (3).

(3) The Minister conducting a review under this section must prepare a report on the result of the review and lay a copy of it before each House of Parliament.

Judges of the European Court of Human Rights

Appointment to European Court of Human Rights

18.(1) In this section "judicial office" means the office of—

(a) Lord Justice of Appeal, Justice of the High Court or Circuit Judge, in England and Wales;

(b) judge of the Court of Session or sheriff, in Scotland;

(c) Lord Justice of Appeal, judge of the High Court or county court judge, in Northern Ireland.

(2) The holder of a judicial office may become a judge of the European Court of Human Rights ("the Court") without being required to relinquish his office.

(3) But he is not required to perform the duties of his judicial office while he is a judge of the Court.

(4) In respect of any period during which he is a judge of the Court—
(a) a Lord Justice of Appeal or Justice of the High Court is not to count as a judge of the relevant court for the purposes of section 2(1) or 4(1) of the Supreme Court Act 1981 (maximum number of judges) nor as a judge of the Supreme Court for the purposes of section 12(1) to (6) of that Act (salaries etc.);
(b) a judge of the Court of Session is not to count as a judge of that court for the purposes of section 1(1) of the Court of Session Act 1988 (maximum number of judges) or of section 9(1)(c) of the Administration of Justice Act 1973 ("the 1973 Act") (salaries etc.);
(c) a Lord Justice of Appeal or judge of the High Court in Northern Ireland is not to count as a judge of the relevant court for the purposes of section 2(1) or 3(1) of the Judicature (Northern Ireland) Act 1978 (maximum number of judges) nor as a judge of the Supreme Court of Northern Ireland for the purposes of section 9(1)(d) of the 1973 Act (salaries etc.);
(d) a Circuit judge is not to count as such for the purposes of section 18 of the Courts Act 1971 (salaries etc.);
(e) a sheriff is not to count as such for the purposes of section 14 of the Sheriff Courts (Scotland) Act 1907 (salaries etc.);
(f) a county court judge of Northern Ireland is not to count as such for the purposes of section 106 of the County Courts Act (Northern Ireland) 1959 (salaries etc.).

(5) If a sheriff principal is appointed a judge of the Court, section 11(1) of the Sheriff Courts (Scotland) Act 1971 (temporary appointment of sheriff principal) applies, while he holds that appointment, as if his office is vacant.

(6) Schedule 4 makes provision about judicial pensions in relation to the holder of a judicial office who serves as a judge of the Court.

(7) The Lord Chancellor or the Secretary of State may by order make such transitional provision (including, in particular, provision for a temporary increase in the maximum number of judges) as he considers appropriate in relation to any holder of a judicial office who has completed his service as a judge of the Court.

Parliamentary procedure

Statements of compatibility

19. — (1) A Minister of the Crown in charge of a Bill in either House of Parliament must, before Second Reading of the Bill —

(a) make a statement to the effect that in his view the provisions of the Bill are compatible with the Convention rights ("a statement of compatibility"); or

(b) make a statement to the effect that although he is unable to make a statement of compatibility the government nevertheless wishes the House to proceed with the Bill.

(2) The statement must be in writing and be published in such manner as the Minister making it considers appropriate.

Supplemental

Orders etc. under this Act

20. — (1) Any power of a Minister of the Crown to make an order under this Act this Act is exercisable by statutory instrument.

(2) The power of the Lord Chancellor or the Secretary of State to make rules (other than rules of court) under section 2(3) or 7(9) is exercisable by statutory instrument.

(3) Any statutory instrument made under section 14, 15 or 16(7) must be laid before Parliament.

(4) No order may be made by the Lord Chancellor or the Secretary of State under section 1(4), 7(11) or 16(2) unless a draft of the order has been laid before, and approved by, each House of Parliament.

(5) Any statutory instrument made under section 18(7) or Schedule 4 or to which subsection (2) applies, shall be subject to annulment in pursuance of a resolution of either House of Parliament.

(6) The power of a Northern Ireland department to make —

(a) rules under section 2(3)(c) or 7(9)(c), or

(b) an order under section 7(11),

is exercisable by statutory rule for the purposes of the Statutory Rules (Northern Ireland) Order 1979.

(7) Any rules made under section 2(3)(c) or 7(9)(c) shall be subject to negative resolution; and section 41 (6) of the Interpretation Act (Northern Ireland) 1954 (meaning of "subject to negative resolution") shall apply as if the power to make the rules were conferred by an Act of the Northern Ireland Assembly.

(8) No order may be made by a Northern Ireland department under section 7(11) unless a draft of the order has been laid before, and approved by, the Northern Ireland Assembly.

Interpretation etc.

21. — (1) In this Act—

"amend" includes repeal and apply (with or without modifications);

"the appropriate Minister" means the Minister of the Crown having charge of the appropriate authorised government department (within the meaning of the Crown Proceedings Act 1947);

"the Commission" means the European Commission of Human Rights;

"the Convention" means the Convention for the Protection of Human Rights and Fundamental Freedoms, agreed by the Council of Europe at Rome on 4th November 1950 as it has effect for the time being in relation to the United Kingdom;

"declaration of incompatibility" means a declaration under section 4;

"Minister of the Crown" has the same meaning as in the Ministers of the Crown Act 1975;

"Northern Ireland Minister" includes the First Minister and the deputy First Minister in Northern Ireland;

"primary legislation" means any —

(a) public general Act;

(b) local and personal Act;

(c) private Act;

(d) Measure of the Church Assembly;

(e) Measure of the General Synod of the Church of England;

(f) Order in Council—

(i) made in exercise of Her Majesty's Royal Prerogative;

(ii) made under section 38(1)(a) of the Northern Ireland Constitution Act 1973 or the corresponding provision of the Northern Ireland Act 1998; or

(iii) amending an Act of a kind mentioned in paragraph (a), (b) or (c);

and includes an order or other instrument made under primary legislation (otherwise than by the National Assembly for Wales, a member of the Scottish Executive, a Northern Ireland Minister or a Northern Ireland department) to the extent to which it operates to bring one or more provisions of that legislation into force or amends any primary legislation;

"the First Protocol" means the protocol to the Convention agreed at Paris on 20th March 1952;

"the Sixth Protocol" means the protocol to the Convention agreed at Strasbourg on 28th April 1983;

"the Eleventh Protocol" means the protocol to the Convention (restructuring the control machinery established by the Convention) agreed at Strasbourg on 11th May 1994;

"remedial order" means an order under section 10;

"subordinate legislation" means any —

(a) Order in Council other than one—

(i) made in exercise of Her Majesty's Royal Prerogative;

(ii) made under section 38(1)(a) of the Northern Ireland Constitution Act 1973 or the corresponding provision of the Northern Ireland Act 1998; or

(iii) amending an Act of a kind mentioned in the definition of primary legislation;

(b) Act of the Scottish Parliament;

(c) Act of the Parliament of Northern Ireland;

(d) Measure of the Assembly established under section 1 of the Northern Ireland Assembly Act 1973;

(e) Act of the Northern Ireland Assembly;

(f) order, rules, regulations, scheme, warrant, byelaw or other instrument made under primary legislation (except to the extent to which it operates to bring one or more provisions of that legislation into force or amends any primary legislation);

(g) order, rules, regulations, scheme, warrant, byelaw or other instrument made under legislation mentioned in paragraph (b), (c), (d) or (e) or made under an Order in Council applying only to Northern Ireland;

(h) order, rules, regulations, scheme, warrant, byelaw or other instrument made by a member of the Scottish Executive, a Northern Ireland Minister or a Northern Ireland department in exercise of prerogative or other executive functions of Her Majesty which are exercisable by such a person on behalf of Her Majesty;

"transferred matters" has the same meaning as in the Northern Ireland Act 1998; and

"tribunal" means any tribunal in which legal proceedings may be brought.

(2) The references in paragraphs (b) and (c) of section 2(1) to Articles are to Articles of the Convention as they had effect immediately before the coming into force of the Eleventh Protocol.

(3) The reference in paragraph (d) of section 2(1) to Article 46 includes a reference to Articles 32 and 54 of the Convention as they had effect immediately before the coming into force of the Eleventh Protocol.

(4) The references in section 2(1) to a report or decision of the Commission or a decision of the Committee of Ministers include references to a report or decision made as provided by paragraphs 3, 4 and 6 of Article 5 of the Eleventh Protocol (transitional provisions).

(5) Any liability under the Army Act 1955, the Air Force Act 1955 or the Naval Discipline Act 1957 to suffer death for an offence is replaced by a liability to imprisonment for life or any less punishment authorised by those Acts; and those Acts shall accordingly have effect with the necessary modifications.

Short title, commencement, application and extent

22. — (1) This Act may be cited as the Human Rights Act 1998.

(2) Sections 18, 20 and 21(5) and this section come into force on the passing of this Act.

(3) The other provisions of this Act come into force on such day as the Secretary of State may by order appoint; and different days may be appointed for different purposes.

(4) Paragraph (b) of subsection (l) of section 7 applies to proceedings brought by or at the instigation of a public authority whenever the act in question took place; but otherwise that subsection does not apply to an act taking place before the coming into force of that section.

(5) This Act binds the Crown.

(6) This Act extends to Northern Ireland.

(7) Section 21(5), so far as it relates to any provision contained in the Army Act 1955, the Air Force Act 1955 or the Naval Discipline Act 1957, extends to any place to which that provision extends.

SCHEDULE 1

[The Articles and Protocols in this schedule are reproduced in *Chapter 3*]

SCHEDULE 2

REMEDIAL ORDERS

Orders

1.—(1) A remedial order may—
- (a) contain such incidental, supplemental, consequential or transitional provision as the person making it considers appropriate;
- (b) be made so as to have effect from a date earlier than that on which it is made;
- (c) make provision for the delegation of specific functions;
- (d) make different provision for different cases.

(2) The power conferred by sub-paragraph (l)(a) includes—
- (a) power to amend primary legislation (including primary legislation other than that which contains the incompatible provision); and
- (b) power to amend or revoke subordinate legislation (including subordinate legislation other than that which contains the incompatible provision).

(3) A remedial order may be made so as to have the same extent as the legislation which it affects.

(4) No person is to be guilty of an offence solely as a result of the retrospective effect of a remedial order.

Procedure

2. No remedial order may be made unless —
   (a) a draft of the order has been approved by a resolution of each House of Parliament made after the end of the period of 60 days beginning with the day on which the draft was laid; or
   (b) it is declared in the order that it appears to the person making it that, because of the urgency of the matter, it is necessary to make the order without a draft being so approved.

Orders laid in draft

3.(1) No draft may be laid under paragraph 2(a) unless —
   (a) the person proposing to make the order has laid before Parliament a document which contains a draft of the proposed order and the required information; and
   (b) the period of 60 days, beginning with the day on which the document required by this sub-paragraph was laid, has ended.

(2) If representations have been made during that period, the draft laid under paragraph 2(a) must be accompanied by a statement containing —
   (a) a summary of the representations; and
   (b) if, as a result of the representations, the proposed order has been changed, details of the changes.

Urgent cases

4. — (1) If a remedial order ("the original order") is made without being approved in draft, the person making it must lay it before Parliament, accompanied by the required information, after it is made.

(2) If representations have been made during the period of 60 days beginning with the day on which the original order was made, the person making it must (after the end of that period) lay before Parliament a statement containing —
   (a) a summary of the representations; and
   (b) if, as a result of the representations, he considers it appropriate to make changes to the original order, details of the changes.

(3) If sub-paragraph (2)(b) applies, the person making the statement must —
   (a) make a further remedial order replacing the original order; and
   (b) lay the replacement order before Parliament.

(4) If, at the end of the period of 120 days beginning with the day on which the original order was made, a resolution has not been passed by each House

approving the original or replacement order, the order ceases to have effect (but without that affecting anything previously done under either order or the power to make a fresh remedial order).

Definitions

5. In this Schedule —

"representations" means representations about a remedial order (or proposed remedial order) made to the person making (or proposing to make) it and includes any relevant Parliamentary report or resolution; and
"required information" means —
  (a) an explanation of the incompatibility which the order (or proposed order) seeks to remove, including particulars of the relevant declaration, finding or order; and
  (b) a statement of the reasons for proceeding under section 10 and for making an order in those terms.

Calculating periods

6. In calculating any period for the purposes of this Schedule, no account is to be taken of any time during which —
  (a) Parliament is dissolved or prorogued; or
  (b) both Houses are adjourned for more than four days.

SCHEDULE 3

['Derogations and Reservations': These are not reproduced. They are explained in *Chapter 3*]

SCHEDULE 4

['Judicial Pensions': Not reproduced]

Appendix II

A Structured Approach

Appendix II: A Structured Approach

Process map A key message arising from the Convention is the need to adopt a structured approach to decision-making. The following map will guide you through the various stages where the Convention is at issue. By asking the following questions in the right order this guide should lead you *to make the right decision and to provide sound reasons in support of it.*

STAGE ONE: IS THE CONVENTION ENGAGED?

• Looking at the facts of the case or the submissions made, is a human right involved?
• If it is not, you can decide the point without further consideration of the Convention so long as you provide reasons for your decision.

STAGE TWO: IDENTIFY THE CONVENTION RIGHT ENGAGED

If a human right *is* engaged, which one is it and what type of right is it?

Absolute Rights
Article 3: the prohibition of torture, inhuman and degrading treatment
Article 4(1): the prohibition of slavery
Article 7: the prohibition of punishment without law

Limited Rights
Article 2: the right to life
Article 4(2): the prohibition on forced labour
Article 5: the right to liberty
Article 6: the right to a fair trial*

Qualified Rights
Article 8: the right to private and family life
Article 9: freedom of thought, conscience and religion*
Article 10: freedom of expression
Article 11: freedom of assembly and association

STAGE THREE: HAS THE CONVENTION BEEN VIOLATED?

• With ABSOLUTE RIGHTS a breach for *any reason* will amount to violation.
• With LIMITED RIGHTS is the restriction on the primary right clearly set out within the limitations or conditions in the Article? If not, there is a violation.
• In the case of QUALIFIED RIGHTS three questions need to be asked. Has the party interfering with the primary right satisfied you that:

1. The restriction is prescribed by clear and accessible domestic law?
2. It pursues a legitimate aim set out in the Article?
3. It is no more than is necessary to secure that legitimate aim (is the measure *proportional*)?

If the answer to *any* of these questions is 'no', there is a violation of the Convention.

STAGE FOUR: IDENTIFY THE 'SOURCE' OF THE VIOLATION

The source of the violation may be a rule of:

- —*primary* national legislation
- —*secondary* national legislation
- —national legal practice or precedent

STAGE FIVE: WHAT DOES THE HUMAN RIGHTS ACT 1998 ALLOW THE COURT TO DO?

In the case of PRIMARY NATIONAL LEGISLATION can you find a possible interpretation which will give effect to the Convention right? If you can, then the law must be applied in this way. In very rare circumstances you may not be able to find a *compatible* interpretation and must instead apply national law as it is. (This is also the position in relation to 'dependent' secondary legislation: see *Chapter 4*)

In the case of SECONDARY NATIONAL LEGISLATION can you find a possible interpretation which will give effect to the Convention right? If you can then the law must be applied in this way. Where you cannot find a *compatible* interpretation you must disregard the national law so as to give effect to the Convention right.

In the case of NATIONAL RULES OF PRACTICE OR PRECEDENT can you find a possible interpretation which will give effect to the Convention right? If you can then the law must be applied in this way. Where you cannot find a *compatible* interpretation you must disregard the national law so as to give effect to the Convention right.

STAGE SIX: RECORD AND ANNOUNCE THE DECISION

- What are the facts of the case as found by the court?
- Why do they lead to the conclusion that you have reached?
- Were any Convention rights involved in arriving at your decision? If so:
  - —Say how they affected your decision
  - —Do this by explaining any or all of the above stages which were relevant to that decision.

Your reasons should always enable you to cross-check that you have reached your decision by the correct route.

---

* As noted in the text, certain aspects of these rights may be *absolute,* see p.38 (right to life) and p.42 (right to *hold* a religious belief). Further advice may be desirable.

Index

An ideal companion to Human Rights and the Courts

Introduction to the
Family Proceedings Court

Elaine Laken
Chris Bazell
Winston Gordon
With a Foreword by Sir Stephen Brown

A basic outline of the law and practice of the family proceedings court in England and Wales produced under the auspices of the Justices' Clerks' Society for use by family panel magistrates and other people interested in the arrangements to provide local justice for children and families. The contents are as follows:

PART ONE
1   Introduction
2   Children
3   Procedures
4   Welfare of the Child
5   Financial Provision
6   Enforcement
7   Domestic Violence and Occupation Orders
8   Adoption

PART TWO
A wide range of practical materials.

Index

Another competence based resource. ISBN 1 872 870 46 5 £13.50 plus £2 p&p.

Waterside Press also publish:

The Sentence of the Court Winston Gordon and Others

The Magistrates Bench Handbook Edited by Bryan Gibson

Introduction to Road Traffic Cases Winston Gordon and Others

Introduction to Criminology Russell Pond

Please ask for details of these and our growing list of specialist publications.

Waterside Press, Domum Road, Winchester SO23 9NN 01962 855567
watersidepress@compuserve.com